## Teacher's guide to book S1

# Contents

CAMBRIDGE
UNIVERSITY PRESS

The following people contributed to the writing of the SMP Interact key stage 3 materials.

| | | | |
|---|---|---|---|
| Ben Alldred | Ian Edney | John Ling | Susan Shilton |
| Juliette Baldwin | Steve Feller | Carole Martin | Caroline Starkey |
| Simon Baxter | Rose Flower | Peter Moody | Liz Stewart |
| Gill Beeney | John Gardiner | Lorna Mulhern | Pam Turner |
| Roger Beeney | Bob Hartman | Mary Pardoe | Biff Vernon |
| Roger Bentote | Spencer Instone | Peter Ransom | Jo Waddingham |
| Sue Briggs | Liz Jackson | Paul Scruton | Nigel Webb |
| David Cassell | Pamela Leon | Richard Sharpe | Heather West |

Others, too numerous to mention individually, gave valuable advice, particularly by commenting on and trialling draft materials.

| Editorial team: | David Cassell | Project administrator: | Ann White |
|---|---|---|---|
| | Spencer Instone | Design: | Melanie Bull |
| | John Ling | | Tiffany Passmore |
| | Mary Pardoe | | Martin Smith |
| | Paul Scruton | Project support: | Carol Cole |
| | Susan Shilton | | Pam Keetch |
| | | | Nicky Lake |
| | | | Jane Seaton |
| | | | Cathy Syred |

Special thanks go to Colin Goldsmith.

PUBLISHED BY THE PRESS SYNDICATE OF THE UNIVERSITY OF CAMBRIDGE
The Pitt Building, Trumpington Street, Cambridge, United Kingdom

CAMBRIDGE UNIVERSITY PRESS
The Edinburgh Building, Cambridge CB2 2RU, UK
40 West 20th Street, New York, NY 10011–4211, USA
10 Stamford Road, Oakleigh, Melbourne 3166, Australia
Ruiz de Alarcón 13, 28014 Madrid, Spain
Dock House, The Waterfront, Cape Town 8001, South Africa

http://www.cambridge.org

© The School Mathematics Project 2001
First published 2001

Printed in the United Kingdom at the University Press, Cambridge

Typeface Minion        System QuarkXPress®

A catalogue record for this book is available from the British Library

ISBN 0 521 79862 0 paperback

Typesetting and technical illustrations by The School Mathematics Project
Photograph by Graham Portlock
Cover image © Tony Stone Images/Darryl Torckler
Cover design by Angela Ashton

# Introduction

## What is distinctive about *SMP Interact*?

*SMP Interact* sets out to help teachers use a variety of teaching approaches in order to stimulate pupils and foster their understanding and enjoyment of mathematics.

A central place is given to discussion and other interactive work. Through discussion with the whole class you can find out about pupils' prior understanding when beginning a topic, can check on their progress and can draw ideas together as work comes to an end. Working interactively on some topics in small groups gives pupils, including the less confident, a chance to clarify and justify their own ideas and to build on, or raise objections to, suggestions put forward by others.

Questions that promote effective discussion and activities well suited to group work occur throughout the material.

*SMP Interact* has benefited from extensive and successful trialling in a variety of schools. The practical suggestions contained in the teacher's guides are based on teachers' experiences, often expressed in their own words.

## Who are Books S1 to S3 for?

Books S1 to S3 follow on from Books 1 and N and cover national curriculum levels up to 6.

## How are the pupils' books intended to be used?

The pupils' books are a resource which can and should be used flexibly. They are not for pupils to work through individually at their own pace. Many of the activities are designed for class or group discussion.

Activities intended to be led by the teacher are shown by a solid strip at  the edge of the pupil's page, and a corresponding strip in the margin of the teacher's guide, where they are fully described.

A broken strip at the edge of the page shows an activity or question in  the pupil's book that is likely to need teacher intervention and support.

Where the writers have a particular way of working in mind, this is stated (for example, 'for two or more people').

Where there is no indication otherwise, the material is suitable for pupils working on their own.

Starred questions (for example, *C7) are more challenging.

### What use is made of software?

Points at which software (on a computer or a graphic calculator) can be used to provide effective support for the work are indicated by these symbols, referring to a spreadsheet, graph plotter or dynamic geometry package respectively. Other suggestions for software support can be found on the SMP's website: www.smpmaths.org.uk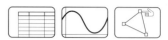

### How is the attainment of pupils assessed?

The interactive class sessions provide much feedback to the teacher about pupils' levels of understanding.

Each unit of work begins with a statement of the key learning objectives and finishes with questions for self-assessment ('What progress have you made?') The latter can be incorporated into a running record of progress.

Revision questions are included in periodic reviews in the pupil's book.

A pack of assessment materials for Books T1, S1 and C1 contains photocopiable masters providing a short assessment for most of the units. Enclosed with the pack is a CD-ROM holding the assessment materials in question bank form so you can compile and edit tests on screen to meet your school's needs. Details of the pack are on the SMP's website.

### What will pupils do for homework?

The practice booklets may be used for homework.

Often a homework can consist of preparatory or follow-up work to an activity in the main pupil's book.

### Answers to questions on resource sheets

For reasons of economy, where pupils have to write their responses on a resource sheet the answers are not always shown in this guide. For convenience in marking you could put the correct responses on a spare copy of each sheet and add it to a file for future use.

# General guidance on teaching approaches

### Getting everyone involved

When you are introducing a new idea or extending an already familiar topic, it is important to get as many pupils as possible actively engaged.

**Posing key questions**
A powerful technique for achieving this is to pose one or two key questions, perhaps in the form of a novel problem to be solved. Ask pupils, working in pairs or small groups, to think about the question and try to come up with an answer.

When everyone has had time to work seriously at the problem (have a further question ready for the faster ones), you can then ask for answers, without at this stage revealing whether they are right or wrong (so that pupils have to keep thinking!). You could ask pupils to comment on each other's answers.

**Open tasks**
Open tasks and questions are often good for getting pupils to think, or thinking more deeply. For example, 'Working in groups of three or four, make up three questions that can be solved using the technique we have just been learning. Try to make your questions as varied as possible.'

## Questioning skills

**Questioning with the whole class**
If your questions to the class are always closed, and you reward the first correct response you get, then you have no way of telling whether other pupils knew the correct answer or whether they had thought about the question at all. It is better to try to get as many pupils as possible to engage with the question, so do not at first say whether an answer is right or wrong. You could ask a pupil how they got their answer, or you could ask a second pupil how they think the first one got their answer.

## Working in groups

**Types of group work**
Group work may be small scale or large scale. In small-scale group work, pupils are asked to work in pairs or small groups for a short while, perhaps to come up with a solution to a novel type of problem before their suggestions are compared. In large-scale group work, pupils carry out in groups a substantial task such as planning a statistical enquiry or designing a poster to get over the essential idea of the topic they have just been studying.

**Organising the groups**
Group size is important. Groups of more than four or five can lead to some pupils making little or no contribution.

For some activities, you may want pupils to work unassisted. But for many, your own contribution will be vital. Then it is generally more effective if, once you are sure that every group has got started, you work intensively with each group in turn.

**After the group work** One way to help pupils feel that they have worked effectively is to get them to report their findings to the whole class. This may be done in a number of different ways. One pupil from each group could report back. Or you could question each group in turn. Or each group could make a poster showing their results.

## Managing discussion

Discussion, whether in a whole-class or group setting, has a vital role to play in developing pupils' understanding. It is most fruitful in an atmosphere where pupils know their contributions are valued and are not always judged in terms of immediate correctness. It needs careful management for it to be effective and teachers are often worried that it will get out of hand. Here are a few common worries, and ways of dealing with them.

**What if ...** '... the group is not used to discussion?'

- Allow time for pupils to work first on the problem individually or in small groups, then they will all have ideas to contribute.

'... everyone tries to talk at once?'

- Set clear rules. For example, pupils raise their hands and you write their name on the board before they can speak.

'... a few pupils dominate whole-class discussion?'

- Precede any class discussion with small-group discussion and nominate the pupils who will feed back to the class.

'... one pupil reaches the end point of a discussion immediately?'

- Tell them that the rest of the group need to be convinced and ask the pupil to convince the rest of the group.

- Accept the suggestion and ask the rest of the group to comment on it.

# Time

| Essential | Optional |
|---|---|
| Sheet 101 | Sheets 98 or 99, and 100<br>OHP transparencies of 98 or 99, and 101 |
| **Practice booklet** pages 3 to 5 | |

## A Happiness graphs (p 4)

Optional: Sheet 98 or 99, and a transparency of the sheet used

◊ Discuss the 'happiness graph'. Happiness is 'measured' on a 0 to 10 scale.

◊ Pupils can draw their own happiness graphs on specially ruled time graph paper (sheet 98 or 99).

*'Very good. I did my own happiness graph on the board for the day I taught the class.'*

**Sheet 98**

can be used to plot a happiness graph for 9 a.m. to 4 p.m.

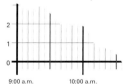

**Sheet 99**

can be used to plot a happiness graph for 9 a.m. to 11 p.m.

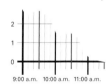

Pupils should label the axes as appropriate, using 12-hour or 24-hour clock times.

◊ Before pupils draw their graphs it may be necessary to establish the times of daily events (e.g. lesson changes, breaks). A transparency of the time graph paper is useful here.

## B Time planner (p 4)

> Optional: Sheet 98 or 99, and a transparency of the sheet used

◊ Discuss the diagram on page 4, posing questions such as 'When does assembly end?', 'How long is break?'

◊ Discuss how you could devise a time plan for a whole week by producing a set of bars, one for each day. Pupils can draw diagrams to show their own timetables (including the weekend if they like). A shorter activity is to produce a diagram for the current day only.

If the whole group has the same timetable, each pupil could do one particular school day and then the days could be collected together to make weekly timetables.

Alternatively, pupils could show how they spend a typical Saturday or Sunday.

As before, they can consider the day from 9 a.m. to 4 p.m. (sheet 98) or from 9 a.m. to 11 p.m. (sheet 99). They can use 12-hour or 24-hour clock times.

## C The 24-hour clock (p 5)

> Optional: Sheet 100

◊ If you haven't already done so in sections A or B, discuss the 12-hour and 24-hour clocks and how to convert time in one form to the other. Point out that 24-hour clock time can be written as, for example, 16:40 or 1640.

Pupils then order the times A to R. They are reproduced as a set of cards on sheet 100: pupils can cut them out and put them in order.

The correct order is B, Q, A, M, R, O, D, G, N, K, L, I, E, C, P, J, F, H.

Pupils could write all the times as a.m./p.m. and then as 24-hour clock times.

Pupils could also work out the time intervals between adjacent cards when they are in order.

◊ A simple game can be played in groups of three:
 • Shuffle the cards and deal six each.
 • Each player plays a card.
 • The latest time (or earliest, or middle, as agreed) wins the trick. The winner of the trick goes first in the next round.

## D How long? (p 6)

**D14** You may need to emphasise that each column shows the times for **one** continuous bus journey.

## E Round trip (p 7)

The task is to find ways of making a round trip starting and finishing at Midtown, visiting all the other places. Bus times and journey times are given.

> Sheet 101, and a transparency of it

◊ You will probably need to work together through one trip. Emphasise that each time is for a **different** bus. For example, there are four buses from Norsey to Budham at the times shown in the box under Norsey.

You can, if you wish, make further conditions (for example, spend at least 30 minutes at each place).

◊ Pupils can check each other's solutions. The shortest possible trips are these.
- M (10:25) E N B S M    6 hours 5 minutes
- M (10:30) B S E N M    6 hours 30 minutes
- M (9:40) E N B S M     6 hours 50 minutes

However, pupils may not find them in the time available.

## F Timetables (p 8)

◊ You may need to emphasise that each column in the timetable shows the times for one continuous bus journey.

You can use the timetable here as the basis for some oral questions similar to the printed questions.

### C The 24-hour clock (p 5)

**C1**
(a) 1430   (b) 1715   (c) 0610
(d) 1225   (e) 2150   (f) 0435
(g) 1825   (h) 2315   (i) 1010
(j) 1940

**C2**
(a) 7:30 a.m.   (b) 4:00 p.m.
(c) 1:45 p.m.   (d) 1:40 a.m.
(e) 12:50 a.m.   (f) 3:15 p.m.
(g) 8:25 a.m.   (h) 12:40 p.m.
(i) 7:55 p.m.   (j) 2:35 p.m.

**C3** 0205, 6:45 a.m., 11:42 a.m., 1:00 p.m., 1600, 8:35 p.m., 9:40 p.m., 2209

## D How long? (p 6)

**D1** (a) 9:30 a.m.  (b) 10:30 a.m.
(c) 1 hour

**D2** (a) 12:20 p.m.  (b) 1:10 p.m.
(c) 50 minutes

**D3** (a) 20 minutes  (b) 50 minutes
(c) 1 hour 10 minutes
(d) 30 minutes

**D4** (a) 1 hour 40 minutes
(b) 2 hours 30 minutes
(c) 2 hours 50 minutes
(d) 1 hour 50 minutes

**D5** (a) 30 minutes  (b) 15 minutes
(c) 1 hour 15 minutes
(d) 1 hour 40 minutes

**D6** 1 hour 40 minutes

**D7** 35 minutes

**D8** 15 minutes

**D9** 35 minutes

**D10** 10 minutes

**D11** 1:45 p.m.

**D12** 3:25 p.m.

**D13** 35 minutes

**D14** (a) 1 hour 15 minutes
(b) 1 hour 40 minutes

**D15** 25 minutes

## F Timetables (p 8)

**F1** 2030 or 8:30 p.m.

**F2** 25 minutes

**F3** 4 minutes

**F4** 22 minutes

**F5** 13 minutes

**F6** The 1934 train

**F7** The 2034 train

**F8** Four trains

**F9** 1956 or 7:56 p.m.

**F10** 1832 or 6:32 p.m.

## What progress have you made? (p 9)

**1** (a) 1500  (b) 1815
(c) 1335  (d) 0905

**2** (a) 5:00 p.m.  (b) 2:20 p.m.
(c) 6:45 a.m.  (d) 10:10 p.m.

**3** 3:30 a.m., 1135, 2:05 p.m., 2340

**4** (a) 45 minutes
(b) 1 hour 20 minutes
(c) 13 hours 20 minutes
(d) 6 hours 25 minutes

**5** 20 minutes

**6** 22 minutes

**7** 1430 or 2:30 p.m.

## Practice booklet

## Sections C and D (p 3)

**1** (a) 1320  (b) 0420  (c) 1150
(d) 1725  (e) 0900  (f) 2330
(g) 2105  (h) 1030

**2** (a) 6:50 a.m.  (b) 1:45 p.m.
(c) 11:10 a.m.  (d) 3:10 p.m.
(e) 4:20 p.m.  (f) 6:35 p.m.
(g) 8:00 p.m.  (h) 10:15 p.m.

**3** (a) 15 minutes  (b) 25 minutes
(c) 55 minutes  (d) 20 minutes
(e) 1 hour 25 minutes or 85 minutes
(f) 1 hour 30 minutes or 90 minutes
(g) 1 hour 30 minutes or 90 minutes
(h) 6 hours 20 minutes

**4** (a) 20 minutes

(b) 1 hour 15 minutes or 75 minutes

(c) 20 minutes

(d) 50 minutes

(e) 2 hours 45 minutes

**5** (a) 45 minutes

(b) 1 hour 20 minutes or 80 minutes

(c) 1 hour 20 minutes or 80 minutes

(d) 45 minutes

(e) 2 hours 15 minutes

(f) 1 hour 20 minutes

**6** (a) 45 minutes

(b) 10 minutes

(c) 1 hour 30 minutes or 90 minutes

## Section F (p 4)

**1** (a) 30 minutes    (b) 25 minutes

(c) 20 minutes    (d) 45 minutes

**2** (a) (i) 0629 or 6:29 a.m.

(ii) 14 minutes

(b) (i) 1445 or 2:45 p.m.

(ii) 25 minutes

(c) 1413 or 2:13 p.m.

(d) 1605 or 4:05 p.m.

(e) 2 hours 1 minute or 121 minutes

(f) (i) 55 minutes

(ii) 1 hour 15 minutes or 75 minutes

(g)

| | |
|---|---|
| Hereford | 2345 |
| Ledbury | 0001 |
| Colwall | 0008 |
| Great Malvern | 0027 |
| Malvern Link | 0030 |
| Foregate St | 0040 |
| Shrub Hill | 0043 |

**Action and result puzzles** (p 10)

In each puzzle, the action cards show operations to be performed on a starting number and the result cards show the results. Pupils match up the results with the actions.

The puzzles provide number practice and an opportunity to apply some logical thinking. They may reveal misconceptions about number.

| Essential | Optional |
|---|---|
| Puzzles on sheets 106 and 107 | Sheet 110 (blank cards) |
| Scissors | Sheets 108 (harder) and 104 (easier) |
| | Transparencies of some sheets, cut into puzzle cards |

**T**

*'I put copies of the games into labelled boxes. I explained what each game was about and allowed them to choose their own games.'*

A selection from the puzzles should be used (listed below roughly in order of difficulty).

Sheet 106    327 puzzle (+ and −, three-digit numbers)
                6.5 puzzle (+ and −, includes simple fractions and decimals)
                3679 puzzle (+ and −, four-digit numbers)

Sheet 107    36 puzzle (+, −, × and ÷, includes simple decimals and negative numbers)
                $q$ puzzle ('logic' puzzle, + and −, two-digit numbers)
                $h$ puzzle ('logic' puzzle, +, −, × and ÷, two-digit numbers)

Pupils who do well with these can do the following as extension.

Sheet 108    16.5 puzzle (+, −, × and ÷, decimals and negative numbers)
                $s$ puzzle ('logic' puzzle, the number $s$ has to be found)
                12 puzzle ($a$, $b$ and $c$ are numbers to be found)

Any pupils who need a gentler start could do the following.

Sheet 104    44 puzzle (+ and −, whole numbers ≤ 100)
                60 puzzle (+, −, × and ÷, simple 2- and 3-digit numbers)
                5.5 puzzle (+ and −, decimals with 0.5 only)

◊   This has worked well with pupils sitting in pairs on tables of four. When each pair had matched the cards, all four pupils discussed what they had done. An aim is to encourage mental number work. However, pupils may want to do some calculations and demonstrate things to their group using pencil and paper. It is not intended that a calculator should be used.

*'I copied the cards on to pieces of acetate which could be moved about on the OHP. Pupils went to the OHP to show how the cards matched up.'*

◊   Puzzles that pupils find easy can be done without cutting out the cards: they simply key each action card to its result card by marking both with the same letter. However, something may be learnt from moving cards around to try ideas out before reaching a final pairing, and some puzzles are almost impossible unless they are done this way.

◊ Solutions can be recorded by
   • keying cards to one another with letters as described above
   • sticking pairs of cards on sheets or in exercise books
   • writing appropriate statements, such as 8 − 3 = 5

◊ After pupils have solved some puzzles, they can make up some of their own (using the blank cards) to try on a partner. This may tell you something about the limits of the mathematics they feel confident with. Some should be able to make up puzzles of the $q$ and $h$ type.

## Sheet 106

### 327 puzzle

| Action | Result |
|--------|--------|
| − 30   | 297    |
| + 40   | 367    |
| − 110  | 217    |
| + 700  | 1027   |
| + 390  | 717    |
| − 89   | 238    |
| + 651  | 978    |
| − 207  | 120    |

### 6.5 puzzle

| Action | Result |
|--------|--------|
| + 2.5  | 9      |
| − 3.5  | 3      |
| + 9    | 15.5   |
| + 2.25 | 8.75   |
| − 0.5  | 6      |
| + 4.75 | 11.25  |
| − $1\frac{1}{2}$ | 5 |
| − $\frac{3}{4}$ | 5.75 |

### 3679 puzzle

| Action  | Result |
|---------|--------|
| + 30    | 3709   |
| − 2030  | 1649   |
| + 45    | 3724   |
| − 95    | 3584   |
| − 2300  | 1379   |
| + 4205  | 7884   |
| + 999   | 4678   |
| − 680   | 2999   |

## Sheet 107

### 36 puzzle

| Action | Result |
|--------|--------|
| ÷ 9    | 4      |
| − 40   | ⁻4     |
| × 3    | 108    |
| + 27   | 63     |
| ÷ 8    | 4.5    |
| × 1.5  | 54     |
| + ⁻50  | ⁻14    |
| ÷ 24   | 1.5    |

$q$ puzzle: $q = 27$

$h$ puzzle: $h = 9$

## Sheet 108 (extension)

### 16.5 puzzle

| Action  | Result |
|---------|--------|
| + 3.5   | 20     |
| ÷ 10    | 1.65   |
| − 17    | ⁻0.5   |
| × ⁻2    | ⁻33    |
| ÷ 0.5   | 33     |
| + ⁻3.5  | 13     |
| − 6.05  | 10.45  |
| × 0.1   | 1.65   |

$s$ puzzle: $s = 4.5$

12 puzzle: $a = 0.5$, $b = 4$ and $c = 2$ (or $b = 2$ and $c = 4$), $d = 10$

## Sheet 104 (gentler start)

### 44 puzzle

| Action | Result |
|--------|--------|
| − 43   | 1      |
| + 43   | 87     |
| − 29   | 15     |
| + 29   | 73     |
| + 50   | 94     |
| − 9    | 35     |
| + 56   | 100    |
| − 14   | 30     |

### 60 puzzle

| Action | Result |
|--------|--------|
| ÷10    | 6      |
| − 10   | 50     |
| − 12   | 48     |
| ÷ 5    | 12     |
| × 3    | 180    |
| × 10   | 600    |
| + 100  | 160    |
| ÷ 3    | 20     |

### 5.5 puzzle

| Action | Result |
|--------|--------|
| + 0.5  | 6      |
| − 0.5  | 5      |
| + 2.5  | 8      |
| − 2.5  | 3      |
| − 1.5  | 4      |
| + 9    | 14.5   |
| + 3.5  | 9      |
| − 3.5  | 2      |

# Chance

This unit introduces probability through games of chance. Probabilities are based on equally likely outcomes and the work here includes equivalent fractions.

| **Essential** | **Optional** |
|---|---|
| Dice, counters<br>Sheets 111 to 115 | OHP transparencies of sheets 114 and 115 |
| **Practice booklet** pages 6 and 7 | |

## A Chance or skill? (p 11)

Dice and counters
Sheets 111 to 113 (game boards)

◊ Before discussing and playing the games, you could get pupils talking about chance, e.g. the National Lottery. People often have peculiar ideas about chance. For example, would they write on a National Lottery ticket the same combination as the one which won last week? If not, why not?

You could ask pupils to think about games they know and to discuss the elements of chance and skill in them.

◊ Before playing each game, ask pupils to try to decide from its rules whether it is a game of pure chance, a game of skill, or a mixture.

Some games of skill give an advantage to the first player. Who goes first is usually decided by a process of chance.

◊ You could split the class into pairs or small groups, with each group playing one of the games and reporting on it.

◊ 'Fours' is a game of skill. 'Line of three' is a mixture of chance and skill. 'Jumping the line' appears to involve skill, because you have to decide which counters to move and it looks as if you can get 'nearer' to winning. But it is a game of pure chance. At any stage there is only one number which will enable the player to win. If any other number comes up, whatever the player does leaves the opponent in essentially the same position.

## B  Fair or unfair? (p 12)

> Dice, counters, sheets 114 and 115
> Optional: Transparencies of sheets 114 and 115

◊ You could start by playing 'Three way race' several times as a class, with a track on the board.

When pupils play the game themselves, ask them to record the results and then pool the class's results.

Let pupils consider each other's ways of making the game fairer (if they can think of any!). Do they agree that they would be fairer?

◊ The first rat race is straightforward (although there may be some pupils who think that 6 is 'harder' to get than other numbers). In the second race you could ask for suggestions for making it fairer, still using two dice. (For example, the track could be shortened for the 'end' numbers; but even so, rat 1 is never going to win!)

For the second rat race, pupils could list possible outcomes to discover that there are more ways to make 7 than there are to make 3, for example. So some scores are more likely than others.

## C Probability (p 13)

◊ Explain first the meanings of the two endpoints of the scale. Something with probability 0 is often described as 'impossible'. However, there are different ways of being impossible and some of them have nothing to do with probability (for example, it is impossible for a triangle to have four sides). So it is better to say 'never happens'. Something with probability 1 always happens, or is certain to happen.

◊ Go through the events listed in the pupil's book and discuss where they go on the scale. The coin example leads to the other especially important point on the scale, $\frac{1}{2}$. Associate this with 'equally likely to happen or not happen', with fairness, 'even chances', etc.

◊ Keep the approach informal. The important thing is to locate a point on the right side of $\frac{1}{2}$, or close to one of the ends when appropriate (for example, in the case of the National Lottery!).

## D Equally likely outcomes (p 14)

◊ A spinner is very useful in connection with probability. It shows fractions in a familiar way.

**D4** If the pupil's answer for (d) is $\frac{1}{3}$, then they have ignored the inequality of the parts.

**Odds**

Although some teachers would like to outlaw 'odds', this language is used a lot in the real world. So it may be better to explain the connection, and the difference, between probability and odds.

Bookmakers' odds make an allowance for profit and are not linked to probability in the simple way shown on the pupil's page. It is only 'fair odds' that are so linked.

## E Equivalent fractions (p 16)

◊ 'Pie' diagrams can be used to explain why the numerator and denominator are both multiplied by the same number. For example, in the case of $\frac{3}{4}$, each of the quarters can be subdivided into, say, 5 equal parts, giving $\frac{15}{20}$ as an equivalent fraction.

◊ You may need to emphasise that equivalence works both ways: $\frac{3}{6}$ is equivalent to $\frac{1}{2}$ and vice versa.

◊ Some pupils may have a tendency to produce a list of equivalent fractions by doubling the numerator and denominator each time, for example:
$$\frac{1}{3} = \frac{2}{6} = \frac{4}{12} = \frac{8}{24} = \cdots$$
Emphasise that this strategy leads to missed fractions, for example $\frac{3}{9}$.

## F Choosing at random (p 18)

◊ In some cultures, raffles and all forms of gambling are disapproved of. But if there are no objections you could simulate a raffle in class.

◊ There are some misconceptions which are worth bringing into the open. Some people think that a 'special' number, like 1 or 100, is less likely to win than an 'ordinary' number (because there are fewer 'special' than 'ordinary' numbers).

**F4** Part (e) assumes knowledge of factors. You may wish to check pupils' knowledge before they try this question.

***F6,7** These questions should lead to discussion. Pupils may not have a strategy for comparing fractions, but may still give valid reasons for their choices. For example, 'B has twice as many reds as A but more than twice as many greens, so it's worse'.

In F7, pupils may say 'Choose D, because it has 3 more greens and only 2 more reds'. The choice is correct but the reasoning is not. Suppose, for example, bag C had 2 green and 1 red and bag D had 5 green and 3 red. The probability of choosing green from C would be $\frac{2}{3}$, and from D $\frac{5}{8}$. $\frac{2}{3}$ is greater than $\frac{5}{8}$, so C would be the better choice.

> 'F6 and F7 were challenging for the top of a middle group but provoked interesting discussion.'

## C Probability (p 13)

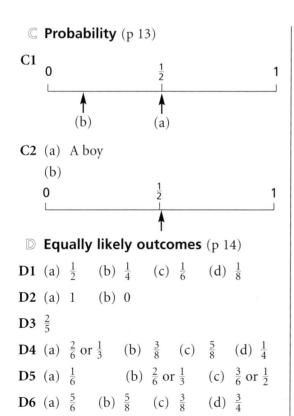

**C1**

**C2** (a) A boy
(b)

## D Equally likely outcomes (p 14)

**D1** (a) $\frac{1}{2}$ (b) $\frac{1}{4}$ (c) $\frac{1}{6}$ (d) $\frac{1}{8}$

**D2** (a) 1 (b) 0

**D3** $\frac{2}{5}$

**D4** (a) $\frac{2}{6}$ or $\frac{1}{3}$ (b) $\frac{3}{8}$ (c) $\frac{5}{8}$ (d) $\frac{1}{4}$

**D5** (a) $\frac{1}{6}$ (b) $\frac{2}{6}$ or $\frac{1}{3}$ (c) $\frac{3}{6}$ or $\frac{1}{2}$

**D6** (a) $\frac{5}{6}$ (b) $\frac{5}{8}$ (c) $\frac{3}{8}$ (d) $\frac{3}{4}$

**D7** $\frac{3}{5}$

**D8** (a) $\frac{2}{3}$ (b) $\frac{1}{8}$ (c) $\frac{4}{9}$ (d) $\frac{7}{10}$ (e) $\frac{1}{2}$

## E Equivalent fractions (p 16)

**E1** $\frac{3}{12}$

**E2** $\frac{2}{10}$

**E3** $\frac{6}{8}, \frac{9}{12}, \frac{12}{16}$

**E4** (a) $\frac{1}{2}$ (b) $\frac{3}{4}$ (c) $\frac{1}{4}$ (d) $\frac{3}{4}$ (e) $\frac{3}{4}$

**E5** (a) $\frac{1}{4}$ (b) $\frac{3}{8}$ (c) $\frac{2}{3}$ (d) $\frac{3}{7}$ (e) $\frac{1}{5}$

**E6** (a) $\frac{2}{3}$ (b) $\frac{5}{8}$ (c) $\frac{2}{5}$
(d) Cannot be simplified (e) $\frac{2}{5}$

**E7** (a) $\frac{1}{3}$ (b) Cannot be simplified (c) $\frac{2}{3}$
(d) Cannot be simplified (e) $\frac{2}{5}$ (f) $\frac{2}{3}$
(g) $\frac{3}{7}$ (h) Cannot be simplified (i) $\frac{5}{8}$
(j) $\frac{4}{15}$

**E8** $\frac{2}{3}$

## F Choosing at random (p 18)

**F1** $\frac{1}{50}$

**F2** $\frac{4}{200} = \frac{1}{50}$

**F3** $\frac{1}{25}$

**F4** (a) $\frac{1}{8}$ (b) $\frac{1}{4}$ (c) $\frac{3}{8}$ (d) $\frac{5}{8}$
(e) $\frac{1}{2}$ (f) $0$ (g) $\frac{3}{4}$

**F5** (a) $\frac{1}{100}$ (b) $\frac{1}{65}$ (c) $\frac{1}{64}$

**\*F6** Sarah should choose bag A.
$\frac{3}{8} = \frac{9}{24}$ $\frac{6}{18} = \frac{1}{3} = \frac{8}{24}$

**\*F7** Dilesh should choose bag D.
$\frac{4}{7} = \frac{48}{84}$ $\frac{7}{12} = \frac{49}{84}$

### What progress have you made? (p 20)

**1** (a)

(b) It never happens.
(c) It always happens (or it is certain).
(d) See diagram.

**2** (a) $\frac{2}{5}$ (b) $\frac{1}{4}$

**3** $\frac{4}{80}$ or $\frac{1}{20}$

**4** (a) $\frac{3}{5}$ (b) $\frac{5}{9}$ (c) $\frac{2}{5}$

## Practice booklet

### Sections D, E and F (p 6)

**1** Spinner A
(a) $\frac{4}{8}$ or $\frac{1}{2}$ (b) $\frac{3}{8}$ (c) $\frac{1}{8}$ (d) $\frac{5}{8}$
Spinner B
(a) $\frac{2}{6}$ or $\frac{1}{3}$ (b) $\frac{1}{6}$ (c) $\frac{3}{6}$ or $\frac{1}{2}$ (d) $\frac{5}{6}$
Spinner C
(a) $\frac{1}{3}$ (b) $\frac{1}{3}$ (c) $\frac{1}{3}$ (d) $\frac{2}{3}$

**2** (a) A (b) A (c) B

**3** Three fractions equivalent to
(a) $\frac{1}{4}$, e.g. $\frac{2}{8}$ $\frac{3}{12}$ $\frac{4}{16}$ $\frac{5}{20}$ $\frac{6}{24}$
(b) $\frac{3}{5}$, e.g. $\frac{6}{10}$ $\frac{9}{15}$ $\frac{12}{20}$ $\frac{15}{25}$ $\frac{18}{30}$
(c) $\frac{5}{8}$, e.g. $\frac{10}{16}$ $\frac{15}{24}$ $\frac{20}{32}$ $\frac{25}{40}$ $\frac{30}{48}$
(d) $\frac{4}{7}$, e.g. $\frac{8}{14}$ $\frac{12}{21}$ $\frac{16}{28}$ $\frac{20}{35}$ $\frac{24}{42}$

**4** (a) $\frac{1}{2}$ (b) $\frac{2}{3}$ (c) $\frac{3}{5}$ (d) $\frac{2}{3}$ (e) $\frac{7}{12}$

**5** (a) $\frac{25}{55}$ Others are equivalent to $\frac{1}{2}$.
(b) $\frac{9}{15}$ Others are equivalent to $\frac{2}{3}$.
(c) $\frac{35}{50}$ Others are equivalent to $\frac{4}{5}$.

**6** (a) $\frac{24}{36} = \frac{2}{3}$ (b) Cannot be simplified
(c) $\frac{30}{140} = \frac{3}{14}$ (d) $\frac{8}{54} = \frac{4}{27}$

**7** (a) $\frac{2}{9}$ (b) $\frac{1}{9}$ (c) $\frac{6}{9}$ or $\frac{2}{3}$
(d) $\frac{6}{9}$ or $\frac{2}{3}$ (e) $\frac{3}{9}$ or $\frac{1}{3}$ (f) $\frac{4}{9}$

**\*8** The probability of an orange sweet
from A is $\frac{3}{9} = \frac{1}{3} = \frac{10}{30}$.
The probability of an orange sweet
from B is $\frac{6}{20} = \frac{3}{10} = \frac{9}{30}$.
So Ann should pick an orange sweet from
A since the probability of picking an
orange sweet from that bag is greater.

**\*9** This table shows the probabilities, and the
bag from which Rick should pick to have
most chance of getting a sweet he likes.
Decimal probabilities have been used to
help comparison, but equivalent fractions
could also be used.

|  | Blue | Blue or yellow |
|---|---|---|
| **Bag P** | 0.3 | 0.6 |
| **Bag Q** | 0.333 | 0.5 |
| **Bag R** | 0.25 | 0.625 |
| **Rick's choice** | Bag Q | Bag R |

# Symmetry

| **Essential** | **Optional** |
|---|---|
| Tracing paper<br>Mirrors<br>Square dotty paper<br>Triangular dotty paper<br>Sheets 117, 120, 121 and 122 | OHP transparency made from sheet 116 |
| **Practice booklet** pages 8 to 11 | |

## A What is symmetrical about these shapes? (p 21)

Discussion should show how much pupils know already about reflection and rotation symmetry.

> Optional: OHP transparency made from sheet 116, tracing paper

◊ One way to generate discussion is for pupils to study the page individually, then discuss it in small groups; then you can bring the whole class together and ask for contributions from the groups.

◊ Most pupils should be able to describe the reflection symmetry of the shapes. Some may realise that shapes with only rotation symmetry (B, C, D, I) are symmetrical in some way but be unable to describe how. Others may know about rotation symmetry already.

*'Good introduction. Many children realise that shapes have symmetry but don't know why. Discussion about each of these shapes helped considerably.'*

## B Rotation symmetry (p 22)

> Tracing paper, sheet 117
> Optional: Square dotty paper

◊ The shape on the page is the first one on sheet 117.

◊ A tracing can be rotated by putting a pencil point at the centre of rotation.

◊ You may wish to explain the convention that having no rotation symmetry is the same as rotation symmetry of order 1. However, this can confuse some pupils at this stage and no use is made of it in this unit.

## C Making designs (p 23)

> Tracing paper, square dotty paper, triangular dotty paper, sheets 120 and 121

C1 You may need to go through the instructions. Check that pupils are rotating the tracing paper to get the new position of the shape. Some may be flipping it over.

◊ Pupils could try the subsequent activities without tracing paper and use tracing paper to check.

## D Rotation and reflection symmetry (p 25)

> Tracing paper, mirrors, sheet 122, square dotty paper

D4 Pupils can extend this by finding all possible ways to shade four squares to produce a design with rotation symmetry.

## E Pentominoes (p 26)

> Tracing paper, mirrors, square dotty paper

## ⓑ Rotation symmetry (p 22)

**B1** Centres of rotation marked on sheet 117

| Shapes with rotation symmetry | Order of rotation symmetry |
|:---:|:---:|
| A | 4 |
| B | 3 |
| C | 2 |
| E | 4 |
| F | 2 |
| G | 3 |
| I | 2 |
| J | 6 |
| K | 8 |
| L | 2 |
| M | 2 |

## ⓒ Making designs (p 23)

**C1**

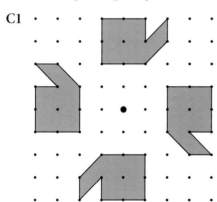

**C2** Completed designs on sheet 120

**C3** (a)

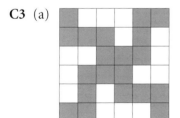

(b)

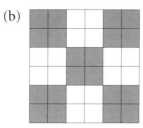

(c)

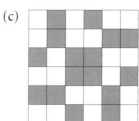

**C4**

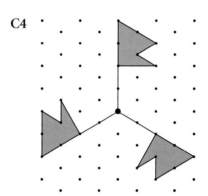

**C5** Completed designs on sheet 121

**C6** (a)         (b)

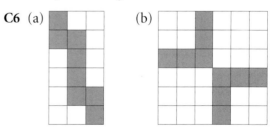

(c)

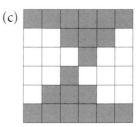

*C7 The pupil's design with rotation symmetry of order 6

## D Rotation and reflection symmetry (p 25)

D1

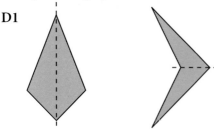

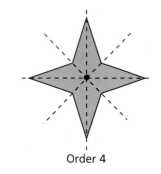

Order 4

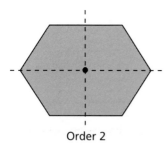

Order 2

**D2 Centres of rotation and lines of symmetry marked on sheet 122**

(a) Rotation symmetry of order 2
No lines of symmetry

(b) Rotation symmetry of order 3
Three lines of symmetry

(c) No rotation symmetry
No lines of symmetry

(d) No rotation symmetry
One line of symmetry

(e) Rotation symmetry of order 3
No lines of symmetry

(f) Rotation symmetry of order 2
Two lines of symmetry

(g) Rotation symmetry of order 2
No lines of symmetry

(h) Rotation symmetry of order 2
Two lines of symmetry

(i) No rotation symmetry
One line of symmetry

(j) No rotation symmetry
No lines of symmetry

(k) Rotation symmetry of order 2
No lines of symmetry

(l) No rotation symmetry
No lines of symmetry

(m) No rotation symmetry
No lines of symmetry

(n) Rotation symmetry of order 2
No lines of symmetry

D3 (a) Order 2

(b) Yes, two lines of symmetry

D4 There are sixteen ways to shade four squares to make a pattern with rotation symmetry (plus twelve that are 90° rotations of some of the sixteen). Pupils have to find eight different ways.

The sixteen ways are shown below.

**Rotation symmetry of order 2**

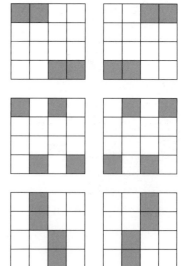

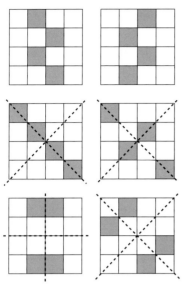

**Rotation symmetry of order 4**

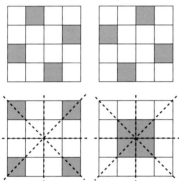

**D5** (a) The pupil's pattern from

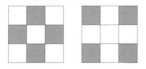

(b) The pupil's pattern from

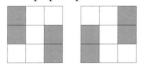

or 90° rotations of these

(c) Some examples are

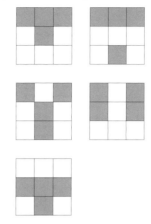

(d) Some examples are

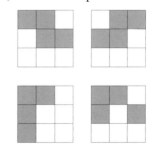

E **Pentominoes** (p 26)

**E1** The pupil's pentomino from

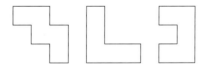

**E2** (a) The pupil's pentomino from

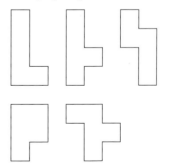

(b) 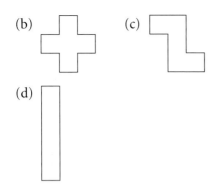 (c)

(d)

**E3** (a) (i)  The pupil's shape; examples are

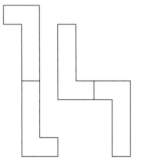

(ii)  The pupil's shape; examples are

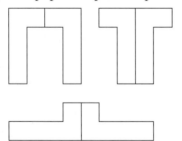

(iii) The pupil's shape; examples are

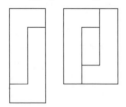

(b)  The pupil's design; examples are

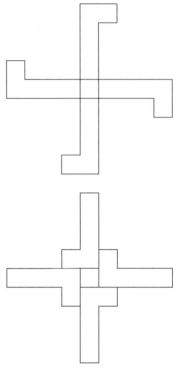

**E4**  The pupil's designs with
   (a)  reflection symmetry but no rotation symmetry
   (b)  rotation symmetry but no reflection symmetry
   (c)  reflection symmetry and rotation symmetry

## What progress have you made? (p 27)

**1** (a)  B and E
   (b)  A
   (c)  C and D

**2**

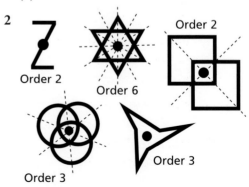

Order 2

Order 2

Order 6

Order 2

Order 3

Order 3

**3** The pupil's pattern; examples are

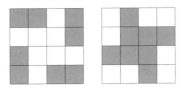

## Practice booklet

### Sections A and B (p 8)

1 Designs A, C and D have rotation symmetry.

2 (a) 5  (b) 8  (c) 2  (d) 4
   (e) 3  (f) 3  (g) 2  (h) 2

### Section C (p 9)

1 The pupil's completed designs with rotation symmetry of order 4

2 The pupil's completed designs with rotation symmetry of order 2

3 The pupil's completed designs with rotation symmetry of order 3

### Sections D and E (p 10)

1 (a) No lines of symmetry
     Rotation symmetry of order 3

  (b) Two lines of symmetry
     Rotation symmetry of order 2

  (c) One line of symmetry
     No rotation symmetry

  (d) No lines of symmetry
     No rotation symmetry

  (e) Two lines of symmetry
     Rotation symmetry of order 2

  (f) No lines of symmetry
     Rotation symmetry of order 3

2 (a) No lines of symmetry
     Rotation symmetry of order 2

  (b) One line of symmetry
     No rotation symmetry

(c) No lines of symmetry
    No rotation symmetry

(d) No lines of symmetry
    Rotation symmetry of order 2

3 (a)

Rotation symmetry of order 4 and 4 lines of symmetry

No rotation symmetry or reflection symmetry

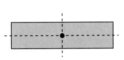
No rotation symmetry and 1 line of symmetry

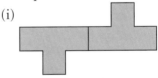
Rotation symmetry of order 2 and 2 lines of symmetry

Rotation symmetry of order 2 and no reflection symmetry

(b) It has one line of reflection symmetry and no rotation symmetry.

(c) Examples are

(i)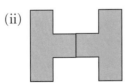

(ii)

(d) The pupil's designs with
   (i) reflection symmetry but no rotation symmetry
   (ii) reflection symmetry and rotation symmetry
   (iii) rotation symmetry of order 4

*4 Symmetry* • **25**

# ⑤ Fractions

Earlier work on fractions, including calculating a fraction of a number, is extended to examples where the fraction is found from a pie chart. Also included are expressing one number as a fraction of another and simplifying fractions.

**Practice booklet** pages 12 to 15

## Ⓐ Revising fractions (p 28)

This provides a diagnostic check that earlier work has been understood.

## Ⓑ Pie charts (p 30)

The pie charts all show simple fractions.

**B11** The amounts are not all whole numbers of pounds because $\frac{1}{12}$ of £30 is £2.50.

**B12** Again, the amounts are not all whole numbers.

## Ⓒ Simplifying fractions (p 32)

This topic has been introduced before, but is likely to need some revision.

## Ⓓ Comparing parts (p 34)

◊ This section highlights the difference between using a fraction to say what proportion something is of a whole and using the idea of ratio to compare the relative sizes of the parts. For example, in question D1 one-third of the members are girls, but the ratio of girls to boys is 1:2.

The use of ratio is very informal here, so you can decide whether to use the colon notation for ratio at this stage. There is a full treatment of ratio in Book S2.

**Puzzles and problems** (p 35)

**E3** Completing the second and third columns requires 'thinking backwards': $\frac{2}{3}$ of a number is 40, so what is the number? This type of thinking is also needed in D5 (unless it is solved by trial and error).

**E4** You can decide whether to allow improper fractions, such as $\frac{3}{2}$.

Ⓐ **Revising fractions** (p 28)

**A1** Sheila is not right because the three parts are not equal. $\frac{1}{4}$ of the square is shaded.

**A2** (a) $\frac{3}{8}$  (b) $\frac{1}{8}$  (c) $\frac{5}{8}$
(d) $\frac{5}{6}$  (e) $\frac{2}{6}$ or $\frac{1}{3}$  (f) $\frac{4}{6}$ or $\frac{2}{3}$

**A3** (a) 15  (b) 5  (c) 4  (d) 3
(e) 6  (f) 6  (g) 2  (h) 8
(i) 9  (j) 7  (k) 3  (l) 5

**A4** (a) 25 kg  (b) 8 cm  (c) 20 g
(d) 9 litres  (e) 7 kg  (f) 12 hectares

**A5** (a) 4  (b) 8  (c) 9  (d) 6
(e) 15  (f) 32  (g) 15  (h) 6

**A6** 12

**A7** $\frac{5}{8}$ of 160 g (100 g) is more than $\frac{3}{4}$ of 120 g (90 g).

**A8** $\frac{3}{8}$ of 240 g (90 g) is more than $\frac{2}{5}$ of 200 g (80 g).

**A9** (a) 79  (b) 158

**A10** (a) 576  (b) 314  (c) 204  (d) 270
(e) 110  (f) 540  (g) 225  (h) 616

**A11** (a) 39 litres  (b) 120 cm  (c) 175 g

Ⓑ **Pie charts** (p 30)

**B1** (a) $\frac{2}{6}$ or $\frac{1}{3}$  (b) $\frac{1}{6}$

**B2** (a) £4  (b) £12  (c) £8

**B3** (a) $\frac{1}{8}$  (b) $\frac{3}{8}$  (c) $\frac{2}{8}$ or $\frac{1}{4}$

**B4** (a) £2  (b) £6  (c) £4

**B5** (a) $\frac{1}{10}$  (b) $\frac{3}{10}$  (c) $\frac{4}{10}$ or $\frac{2}{5}$

**B6** (a) 3  (b) 9  (c) 12

**B7** (a) $\frac{1}{8}$  (b) $\frac{5}{8}$  (c) $\frac{2}{8}$ or $\frac{1}{4}$

**B8** (a) 20  (b) 8

**B9** 18

**B10** 14

**B11** (a) £10  (b) £12.50  (c) £7.50

**B12** (a) 62.5 ha  (b) 312.5 ha  (c) 125 ha

Ⓒ **Simplifying fractions** (p 32)

**C1** $\frac{4}{6} = \frac{2}{3}$

**C2** (a) $\frac{1}{2}$  (b) $\frac{1}{5}$  (c) $\frac{1}{3}$  (d) $\frac{3}{5}$  (e) $\frac{2}{3}$

**C3** (a) $\frac{3}{4}$  (b) $\frac{2}{3}$  (c) $\frac{5}{8}$  (d) $\frac{3}{10}$  (e) $\frac{1}{4}$

**C4** $\frac{1}{4}$

**C5** $\frac{1}{3}$

**C6** $\frac{1}{3}$

**C7** $\frac{3}{4}$

**C8** (a) $\frac{2}{5}$  (b) $\frac{3}{8}$  (c) $\frac{2}{5}$

**C9** $\frac{3}{5}$

**C10** (a) $\frac{5}{8}$  (b) $\frac{1}{4}$  (c) $\frac{1}{8}$

**C11** $\frac{3}{7}$

Ⓓ **Comparing parts** (p 34)

**D1** (a) $\frac{1}{3}$  (b) $\frac{2}{3}$

**D2** (a) $\frac{1}{4}$
(b) There are **three** times as many women in the pool as men.

**D3** (a) $\frac{4}{5}$

(b) She won **four** times as many matches as she lost.

**D4** (a) $\frac{1}{6}$   (b) $\frac{5}{6}$   (c) 7   (d) 35

**D5** There are three times as many red beads as green beads.

**D6** (a) 40      (b) 160

**D7** $\frac{2}{5}$

### E Puzzles and problems (p 35)

**E1** (a) $\frac{1}{3}$ of 24   (b) $\frac{3}{4}$ of 40   (c) $\frac{3}{4}$ of 36
(d) $\frac{1}{3}$ of 36 and $\frac{2}{5}$ of 30
(e) $\frac{1}{3}$ of 30 and $\frac{2}{5}$ of 25
(f) $\frac{2}{3}$ of 24 and $\frac{2}{5}$ of 40

**E2** He has one gold piece left.

**E3**

|  | 12 | 36 | 60 |
|---|---|---|---|
| $\frac{1}{4}$ of | 3 | 9 | 15 |
| $\frac{1}{6}$ of | 2 | 6 | 10 |
| $\frac{2}{3}$ of | 8 | 24 | 40 |

**E4** Proper fractions: $\frac{1}{2}$ $\frac{1}{3}$ $\frac{1}{4}$ $\frac{1}{6}$ $\frac{2}{3}$ $\frac{3}{4}$
Improper fractions: $\frac{2}{1}$ $\frac{3}{1}$ $\frac{4}{1}$ $\frac{6}{1}$ $\frac{3}{2}$ $\frac{4}{3}$

(and $\frac{1}{1}$ if a digit can be repeated)

**E5** 32 trees

### What progress have you made? (p 36)

**1** (a) 18      (b) 12

**2** (a) $\frac{1}{4}$      (b) 8

**3** (a) $\frac{7}{8}$      (b) $\frac{7}{10}$      (c) $\frac{3}{10}$

**4** $\frac{3}{5}$

## Practice booklet

## Section A (p 12)

**1** (a) 8   (b) 4   (c) 5   (d) 4
(e) 6   (f) 4   (g) 5   (h) 4

**2** (a) 8   (b) 10   (c) 12   (d) 18
(e) 18   (f) 24   (g) 10   (h) 12

**3** (a) 16   (b) 24   (c) 30   (d) 15   (e) 27

**4** (a) $\frac{3}{8}$ of 240 g      (b) $\frac{3}{5}$ of 60 sweets
(c) $\frac{5}{7}$ of £140      (d) $\frac{3}{4}$ of 840 km²

**5** (a) 369   (b) 430   (c) 469   (d) 87
(e) 365   (f) 710   (g) 276   (h) 252
(i) 336   (j) 243   (k) 198   (l) 231

## Section B (p 13)

**1** (a) (i) $\frac{5}{8}$      (ii) $\frac{1}{4}$ or $\frac{2}{8}$
(b) (i) 5      (ii) 25

**2** (a) 4 h      (b) 8 h      (c) 16 h

**3** (a) 4 kg      (b) 8 kg      (c) 20 kg

## Sections C and D (p 14)

**1** (a) $\frac{1}{4}$   (b) $\frac{1}{4}$   (c) $\frac{1}{5}$   (d) $\frac{1}{6}$
(e) $\frac{4}{5}$   (f) $\frac{2}{3}$   (g) $\frac{3}{4}$   (h) $\frac{2}{3}$
(i) $\frac{5}{6}$   (j) $\frac{5}{6}$   (k) $\frac{5}{8}$   (l) $\frac{3}{4}$

**2** (a) $\frac{2}{3}$   (b) $\frac{5}{8}$   (c) $\frac{3}{5}$

**3** $\frac{5}{9}$

**4** (a) $\frac{2}{3}$   (b) **Twice** as many pupils walk to school as do not.

**5** (a) $\frac{7}{8}$   (b) **Seven** times as many are doing front crawl as are not.

## Section E (p 15)

**1**

|  | 24 | 48 | 72 |
|---|---|---|---|
| $\frac{1}{8}$ of | 3 | 6 | 9 |
| $\frac{1}{3}$ of | 8 | 16 | 24 |
| $\frac{3}{4}$ of | 18 | 36 | 54 |

**2** 65

**3** (a) 192      (b) 144      (c) 40
(d) 7      (e) 1

**4** (a) 10      (b) 5      (c) 4
(d) 1, which can be returned to the neighbour!
$\frac{1}{2} + \frac{1}{4} + \frac{1}{5} = \frac{19}{20}$, not a whole 1,
so this 'trick' gives them slightly more than the will intended.

# ⑥ Number grids

In this unit, pupils solve number grid problems using addition and subtraction. This includes using the idea of an inverse operation ('working backwards').

Algebra arises through investigating number grids. Pupils simplify expressions such as $n + 4 + n - 3$ and produce simple algebraic proofs of general statements.

---

**Optional**

A4 sheets of paper
Felt-tip pens or crayons
Squared paper

**Practice booklet** pages 16 to 20

---

## Ⓐ Square grids (p 37)

The idea of a number grid is introduced. There are many opportunities to discuss mental methods of addition and subtraction.

> Optional: Squared paper is useful for drawing grids; A4 sheets of paper and felt-tip pens or crayons (for *Human number grids*)

## Human number grids

**T**

This introductory activity does not appear in the pupil material.

◊ Each pupil or pair of pupils represents a position in a number grid. (Number grids are on page 37 of the pupil's book.)

Each position will contain a number. (For pupils familiar with spreadsheets, the idea of a 'cell' may help.)

The operations used are restricted to addition and subtraction.

◊ Tables/desks need to be arranged in rows and columns so that the cells form a grid. Explain, with appropriate diagrams, that the class is going to form a human number grid that uses rules to get from a number in one cell to a number in another. A possible diagram is shown below.

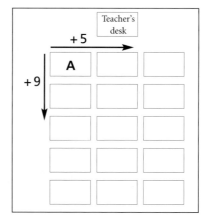

◊ Referring to the numbers is easier if the cells are labelled.
Pupils can discuss how each cell might be labelled, for example:

  • A1, A2, B1, … as on a spreadsheet

  • A, B, C, …

  • or with the pupils' names

◊ Initially, it may be beneficial to use only addition or use sufficiently large numbers in cell A to avoid the complication of negative numbers.

◊ Decide on the first pair of rules and ask the pupils in the cell marked A in the diagram to choose a number for that cell.
Discuss how the numbers in other cells are found.
Now ask the pupils in cell A to choose another number, write it on both sides of a sheet of paper and hold it up.
Pupils now work out what number would be in their cell, write it on both sides of their sheet of paper and hold it up.
This can be repeated with different pupils deciding on the number for their cell.

◊ Questions can be posed in a class discussion, for example:
  - Suppose the number in Julie and Asif's cell is 20.
    What number is in your cell, Peter?
    What number will be in Jenny's cell?
  - What number do we need to put in cell A so that
    the number in cell F is 100?
  - Find a number for cell A so that the number in cell K is negative.
  - What happens if the 'across' and 'down' rules change places?

Ask pupils to explain how they worked out their answers. You could
introduce the idea of an 'inverse' and encourage more confident pupils to
use this word in their explanations.

## Square grids

◊ Point out that all grids in the unit are square grids.

◊ One teacher presented unfinished grids on an OHP transparency and
asked for volunteers to fill in any empty square. She found that less
confident pupils chose easy squares to fill in while 'others with more
confidence chose the hardest, leading to class discussion, and the idea of a
"diagonal" rule came out naturally.'

◊ In one school, the class looked at rules in every
possible direction as shown in the diagram.

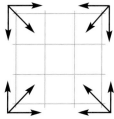

*'Many were surprised by
the fact that there was
more than one route from
one square to another,
giving the same answer.'*

◊ In discussion, bring out the fact that there are different ways to calculate a
number in a square depending on your route through the grid. For
example, the number in the bottom right-hand square in a 3 by 3 grid
can be reached in six different ways. Pupils can try to find all these ways.
Investigating the number of different routes through a grid to each square
can lead to work on Pascal's triangle.

A1 In part (b), make sure pupils realise that the diagonal rule fits any
position on these grids and not just those on the leading diagonal.
In part (c), some pupils may continue to use the '+ 6' and '+ 2' rules here.
Discuss why using the diagonal rule '+ 8' could be used to give the same
result.

A2 In part (b), emphasise that the diagonal rule fits any position on the grid.

A3 It is very likely that negative numbers will appear in the grids, providing
an opportunity to consolidate work on negative numbers. However, if
you want to try to avoid this, you could suggest that pupils choose quite
large numbers for the top left-hand square of their grids or stick to rules
that involve addition only.

Appropriate teacher input is important here. Pupils could:
- consider rules that involve addition only
- choose two rules and investigate grids that use those rules only
- consider rectangular grids

Some pupils will easily see the link between the across, down and diagonal rules and can move quickly on to question A4.

**A4** Some pupils may need to enter numbers in the grid to find the diagonal rules. Encourage pupils to use the results of their investigation in A3 to calculate the diagonal rules from the across and down rules only.

**A5** Some pupils can look for all possible pairs, introducing the idea of an infinite number of pairs of the forms
- '+ $a$' and '+ $(11 - a)$' in part (a)
- '+ $b$' and '+ $(4 - b)$' in part (b)

## Ⓑ **Grid puzzles** (p 39)

◊ For B1 to B3, emphasise that it is not necessary to complete the whole grid to solve the puzzle, just find the missing number or rules.

◊ Encourage pupils to use the word 'inverse' to describe their methods.

**B3** As a possible extension, pupils could make up their own puzzles like this to solve. However, puzzles without at least one pair of numbers in the same horizontal or vertical row (like (f)) are easy to construct but more difficult to solve. These may provide an enjoyable challenge, but if they lead to frustration, pupils could be restricted to making up puzzles with at least one pair of numbers in the same horizontal or vertical row.

Pupils could solve puzzle (f) using trial and improvement or possibly by the following more direct method.

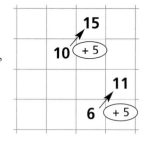

The rule in this diagonal direction ( ↗ ) is '+ 5' so the number in the top row directly above the 6 is 10 + 5 = 15.

Now the down rule is easily found to be '– 3' and the across rule is '+ 2'.

This method can be adapted for the problems in B5 (adding more rows and columns to the grid where necessary).

*B5 Pupils can devise their own methods to solve these. Encourage them to be systematic and ask them to explain their methods to you or each other. Some individuals may be able to solve these problems using a direct method such as the one above. Others may devise systematic trial and improvement methods.

**B6** Encourage pupils to be systematic in their choice of pairs to make the link easier to find. The link could be expressed in words: for example, 'If the across rule is to add a number, then the down rule is to subtract twice that number'.

## ⓒ **Algebra on grids** (p 41)

Algebra is introduced in the context of number grids.

◊ The teacher-led introduction begins with a grid that uses addition only. After discussion of this grid, you may wish pupils to try questions C1 to C3 where the rules are restricted to addition. Then move on to the second grid on page 41 and to questions C4 to C6.
You may find a number line is helpful in getting these ideas across.

Remind pupils of earlier work in section A on finding rules. Emphasise that the expressions in the grid show how to find any number on the grid **directly** from the top left corner. For example, as the expression in the bottom right corner is $n + 14$, then the rule to go from the number in the top left square to the number in the bottom right square is '+ 14'.

In the second grid, pupils who suggest '$h - 9$' for the square below '$h - 2$' are possibly thinking of '$h - 2 + 7$' as '$h - (2 + 7)$'. Discussion of numerical examples may help to clear up any confusion.

Ensure that pupils understand, for example, that '$h + 7 - 4$' gives the same result as '$h - 4 + 7$'.

**C2** Emphasise that the expression in the bottom right square gives a direct method of finding these numbers.

## Ⓓ **Grid investigations** (p 43)

**D1** In part (b) you may need to emphasise that the across and down rules must add and take away the **same** number.

◊ D3 to D6 provide an opportunity for more able pupils to choose to use algebra for themselves to explain their findings.

After pupils have investigated opposite corners for themselves, draw their conclusions together in a discussion that leads to the algebraic ideas in section E.

## Ⓔ **Using algebra** (p 45)

◊ The teacher-led discussion of the use of algebra leads directly from the pupils' investigations in questions D3 to D6.

Ensure that pupils are aware that finding the expression for the opposite corners total to be $2n + 6$ each time proves that the totals will be the same for any value of $n$ and also gives the rule to find this total.
Extend your discussion to consider how to simplify expressions such as $n - 3 + n - 4$ and $n + n + 2 + n - 3$.

**E3** This gives an opportunity to emphasise the fact that equivalent expressions are equal for **all** values of the variables and not just a selected few.

**Extension** Pupils could find and prove that the opposite corners total on a 3 by 3 grid is 2 times the centre number or that the diagonals total is 3 times the centre number.

## Ⓐ Square grids (p 37)

**A1** (a)  The pupil's grids

(b)  The rule is '+ 8', with the pupil's explanations.

(c)  (i)

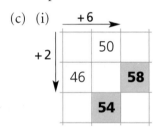

(ii)

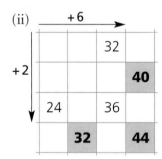

A2 (a) (i)

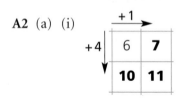

(ii)

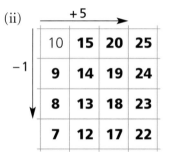

(iii)

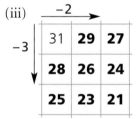

(b)  (i) + 5    (ii) + 4    (iii) − 5
with the pupil's explanation

**A3**  The pupil's investigation and description of the link

**A4** (a)  + 17    (b)  + 5

**A5** (a)  The pupil's pairs of rules equivalent to '+ 11', for example,

across '+ 1', down '+ 10'
or across '+ 5', down '+ 6'

(b)  The pupil's pairs of rules equivalent to '+ 4', for example,

across '+ 1', down '+ 3'
or across '− 1', down '+ 5'

## B Grid puzzles (p 39)

**B1** (a) 23* (b) 30* (c) 39

(d) 25 (e) 43 (f) 95

*Pupils who have not grasped the idea that the rules operate from left to right and from top to bottom might give 27 and 90 as their answers for parts (a) and (b) respectively.

**B2** (a) Across '+ 4', down '+ 9'

(b) Across '– 4', down '– 2'

(c) Down '+ 5'   (d) Down '– 3'

(e) Down '+ 21'   (f) Across '– 5'

**B3** (a) Across '+ 3', down '+ 8'

(b) Across '+ 7', down '– 3'

(c) Across '– 3', down '– 4'

(d) Across '– 2', down '+ 11'

(e) Across '– 5', down '– 3'

(f) Across '+ 2', down '– 3'

**B4** (a) (f) is usually the most difficult.

(b) The pupil's reasons

*\***B5** (a) Across '+ 1', down '+ 2'

(b) Across '+ 6', down '– 2'

(c) Across '– 1', down '+ 4'

*\***B6** (a) The pupil's pairs of rules,
for example,
across '+ 1', down '– 2'
or across '– 4', down '+ 8'

(b) The pupil's descriptions of the link,
for example,

'If the across rule is to add a number, then the down rule is to subtract twice that number.'

'If the across rule is to subtract a number, then the down rule is to add twice that number.'

## C Algebra on grids (p 41)

**C1** (a)

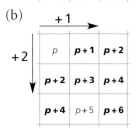

(b)

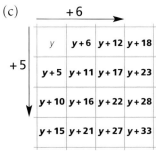

(c)

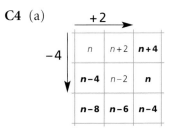

**C2** (a) 114   (b) 106   (c) 133

**C3** (a) Across '+ 6', down '+ 5'

(b) Across '+ 5', down '+ 1'

(c) Across '+ 3', down '+ 10'

**C4** (a)

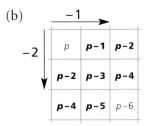

(b)

(c)

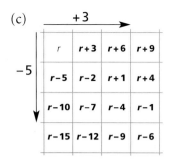

**C5** (a) 54 (b) 56 (c) 56

**C6** (a) $f + 11$ (b) $y + 12$ (c) $x + 6$
(d) $z - 10$ (e) $p + 1$ (f) $m - 3$
(g) $q + 3$ (h) $w - 14$ (i) $h + 5$

Ⓓ **Grid investigations** (p 43)

**D1** (a) (i)

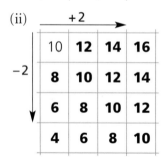

(ii)

(iii)

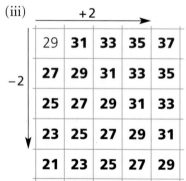

(b) The pupil's investigation

(c) The pupil's observations about symmetry and diagonals

**D2** (a)

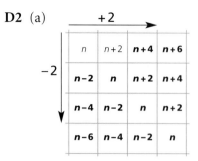

(b) The pupil's explanation, for example, the expression in both those squares is the same ($n$) so the numbers will be the same.

(c) The pupil's observations, for example, the numbers in any diagonal going down from left to right are the same.

**D3** (a) $37 + 13 = 50$ (b) The pupil's grids

(c) For each grid, the opposite corners totals are the same – this result could be explained using algebra.

**D4** The pupil's investigation

**D5** (a)

| Opposite corners table | |
|---|---|
| Top left number | Opposite corners total |
| 2 | 10 |
| 3 | 12 |
| 4 | 14 |
| 10 | 26 |

(b) The pupil's grids and results

(c) 'The opposite corners total is the top left number times 2 and add 6' or '… (the top left number $\times$ 2) + 6' or '… (the top left number + 3) $\times$ 2' or '… $2n + 6$' or equivalent.

(d) 206

**D6** The pupil's investigation

## E Using algebra (p 45)

**E1** Grid P

(a)

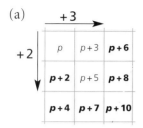

(b) Both pairs of corners add up to $2p + 10$.

(c) Yes

(d) 210

Grid N

(a)

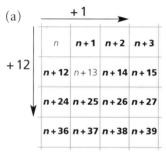

(b) Both pairs of corners add up to $2n + 39$.

(c) Yes

(d) 239

Grid T

(a)

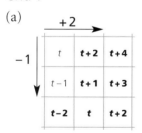

(b) Both pairs of corners add up to $2t + 2$.

(c) Yes

(d) 202

**E2** A and I, B and G, C and E, D and H

**E3** The pupil's explanation, for example, the expressions have the same value for **one** value of $n$ but this does not mean that the expressions have the same value for **all** values for $n$.

**E4**
(a) $2p + 6$      (b) $2y + 9$
(c) $3q + 8$      (d) $3t + 4$
(e) $2x + 1$      (f) $3r + 6$
(g) $2w - 9$      (h) $2j - 1$
(i) $3h - 2$

**E5** The pupil's investigation

### What progress have you made? (p 47)

1

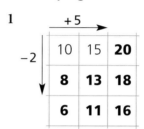

2 5

3 (a) Across '+ 5'
   (b) Across '+ 6', down '− 2'
   (c) Across '− 5', down '− 3'
   (d) Across '− 4', down '+ 1'

4 (a) $n + 7$    (b) $p + 6$    (c) $y - 7$
   (d) $t - 3$    (e) $2h + 3$    (f) $3v - 11$

### Practice booklet

### Sections A and B (p 16)

1 (a) (i)

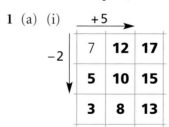

(ii)

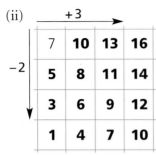

(iii)

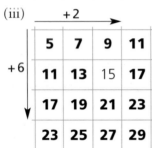

(iv)

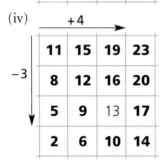

    (b)  (i)  + 3  (ii)  + 1  (iii) + 8  (iv) + 1

**2** (a)  + 13        (b)  + 2

## Section C (p 17)

**1** (a)  (i)

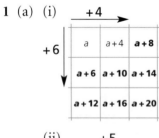

    (ii)

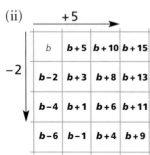

       (b)  (i)   120         (ii)  109

       (c)  (i)   80          (ii)  91

**2** (a)  Across '+ 3', down '+ 4'

    (b)  Across '+ 5', down '+ 3'

    (c)  Across '– 1', down '+ 4'

**3** (a)  $t + 11$    (b)  $a + 7$    (c)  $q + 6$

    (d)  $p + 4$    (e)  $x + 10$   (f)  $y + 2$

    (g)  $s - 4$    (h)  $v - 5$    (i)  $b + 6$

    (j)  $a - 4$    (k)  $f - 16$   (l)  $c + 2$

    (m) $d - 11$   (n)  $g - 2$    (o)  $h - 14$

## Sections D and E (p 18)

**1** (a)

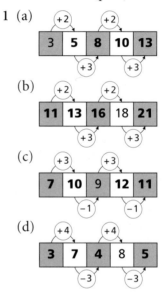

    (b)

    (c)

    (d)

**2** (a)  + 4  (b)  + 7  (c)  + 8  (d)  + 4

**3** The pupil's pairs of rules, for example,

    top '+ 1', bottom '+ 3'

    or top '+ 2', bottom '+ 2'

    or top '+ 3', bottom '+ 1'

    or top '+ 5', bottom '– 1'

**4** (a)

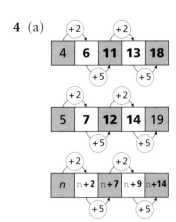

(b)

| End total table | |
|---|---|
| First number | End total |
| 3 | 20 |
| 4 | 22 |
| 5 | 24 |
| $n$ | $2n + 14$ |

(c) 'The end total is
2 times the first number add 14' or
'... (the first number $\times$ 2) + 14' or
'... (the first number + 7) $\times$ 2' or
'... $2n + 14$ where $n$ is the first number'
or equivalent.

(d) 30

**5** The pupil's investigation

**6** A and D, C and I, E and G

**7** (a) $2p + 3$    (b) $3y + 9$    (c) $2q + 10$
   (d) $2t + 3$    (e) $2x + 2$    (f) $3r + 6$
   (g) $2w - 13$    (h) $2j - 3$    (i) $2h - 6$

**8** (a)

| Grid total table | |
|---|---|
| Top left | Grid total |
| 2 | 63 |
| 3 | 72 |
| 4 | 81 |

(b) 'The grid total is 9 times the top left number add 45' or
'... (the top left number $\times$ 9) + 45' or
'... (the top left number + 5) $\times$ 9' or
'... $9n + 45$ where $n$ is the top left number'
or equivalent.

(c) 495

**9** The pupil's investigation

# **7 Perpendicular and parallel lines**

In several places here, letters are used to label points, then line segments or polygons are referred to in terms of those letters. Some pupils find this convention difficult, but it is an indispensable one and it is important to help them feel comfortable with it.

---

**Essential**

Set square
Squared paper

**Practice booklet** pages 21 to 24

---

## Ⓐ **Right angles** (p 48)

For some pupils, this section will be revision.

Set square

**A2** Some pupils may be uncertain about the points of the compass and find it difficult to relate them to turning; clockwise and anticlockwise may also be a problem. If so, it's worth developing this question into a class activity. Establish what direction is north in relation to your classroom. Then pupils take turns to stand facing a given direction, follow instructions to turn clockwise or anticlockwise through a right angle and then say what direction they are now facing.

**A4** You can develop this question and A5 into class discussion if pupils seem likely to benefit from it.

*'Good practice with using a ruler and set square.'*

**A6** An aim here is to develop accuracy. You can introduce the idea of measuring both diagonals of a rectangle to check its 'squareness'.

## Ⓑ **The shortest route to a line** (p 51)

Set square, squared paper

**T**

*'NONE of the class realised that the shortest line was the perpendicular and I had to class-teach it .'*

◊ Many pupils find it difficult to see that the shortest path from a point to a line is perpendicular to the line. When they have drawn point H and the line AB (the exact positions don't matter), you can ask them to draw the shortest route; they can then challenge their neighbour to draw a shorter route than theirs. The angle each drawn route makes with AB can be measured. This may lead to further drawing and angle measuring.

◊ A complementary approach is to draw this
on a transparency and display it on the OHP.
Ask how to draw the line from H to line AB.
Most pupils should have no difficulty in saying
'straight down', so you can draw the path, point to one of the angles it
makes with AB and ask the size of the angle. The answer 'a right angle'
should be forthcoming. Check that everybody agrees.

You can then turn the acetate round like this
and ask what the angle is now. If any pupils hesitate,
move the acetate back so AB is 'horizontal' again
and check they can say what the angle is. Move AB
back to its oblique position and get them to tell you whether
anything has happened to change the angle between the path and AB,
and so on ...

## ℂ **Parallel lines** (p 52)

> Squared paper

◊ Some pupils will have met the word 'parallel' before, so you could begin
by asking someone to draw a pair of parallel lines on the board and
asking the rest of the class what it is that makes the lines parallel. Ideas
such as 'they never meet', 'they go in the same direction' and 'they stay the
same distance apart' may arise. Clarify that parallel lines do not have to be
the same length or lined up in some special way. At the same time you
can ask about where parallel lines occur in the real world.

The word 'parallel' is restricted to straight lines here, though it is used in
everyday language to refer to curved lines (rails on a railway, lines of
latitude) that never meet.

**C3** To identify a set of parallel lines, some pupils may need help to see that
that lines are all made up of segments that go, for example, one square
across and two squares up.

## 𝔸 **Right angles** (p 48)

**A1** 90°

**A2** (a) North        (b) North-east

    (c) North-east

**A3** (a) The angles between them (56° and
34°) add up to 90°.

    (b) $a$ and $h$, $b$ and $d$

**A4** 2 o'clock

**A5** Ten to nine (8:50)

**A6** The pupil's drawing of the rectangle

**A7** The pupil's drawing (the fourth side
should be 11 cm long)

**A8** The pupil's drawing (the missing sides
should be 2.7 cm and 7.2 cm long)

**A9** The pupil's drawing

**A10** $b$ and $f$

**A11** $q$ and $v$

**A12** $d$ and $e$, $f$ and $i$, $g$ and $h$

**B1** (a)

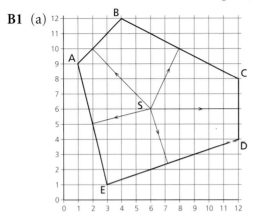

(b) The swimmer should swim
to edge ED.

**B2** (a)

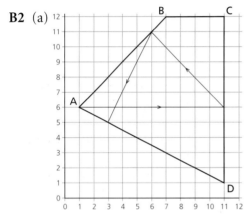

(b) She gets to the point (3, 5).

Ⓒ **Parallel lines** (p 52)

**C1** They are parallel. In each case, for every
3 squares to the right the line goes 2
squares down.

**C2** The pupil's drawing; the first line should
go through P and (4, 3) and the second
through Q and (6, 9).

**C3** $a$, $b$, $h$ and $j$; $c$, $i$ and $k$; $d$, $f$ and $g$; $e$ and $l$

**C4**

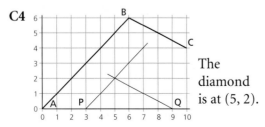

The
diamond
is at (5, 2).

**C5**

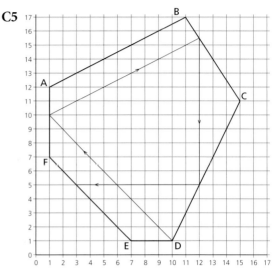

The treasure is buried at (3, 5).

**C6** The two lengths measured on each
transversal are the same.
If you mark points 12 cm apart and 4 cm
apart, the lengths measured on each
transversal are in the ratio 2 : 1.
In general, if the distances between the
dots on the parallel lines are in the ratio
$n$ : 1, the lengths measured on each
transversal are in the ratio $n - 1$ : 1.

**C7** (a) Opposite sides are equal.
Opposite angles are equal.

(b) It has rotation symmetry of order 2.

(c) It does not have reflection symmetry
(unless a rhombus happens to have
been drawn).

(d) A parallelogram

**C8** (a) All four sides are equal.

(b) Order 2

(c) Each of the diagonals is a line of
reflection symmetry.

(d) A rhombus

**C9** (a) Opposite sides are equal.

(b) All four angles are right angles.

(c) It has two lines of symmetry going
through its centre, parallel to the
sides.

(d) A rectangle

## What progress have you made? (p 56)

1  *a* and *b*, *c* and *d*, *e* and *f*

2  The pupil's drawing

3  The pupil's drawing of two parallel lines 4 cm apart.

4  (a) and (b)

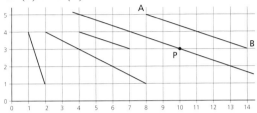

The line from (4, 4) to (7, 3) is parallel to AB.

## Practice booklet

### Sections A and B (p 21)

1  (a)  South          (b)  South-east

2  49°, 23° and 18°

3  *a* and *d*, *b* and *h*, *c* and *f*

4  (a), (b) and (c)

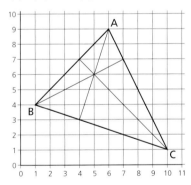

(d)  All three pass through one point.

5  (a) and (b)

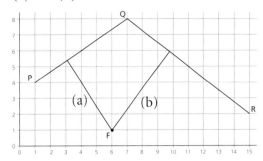

## Section C (p 23)

1  *a* and *c*, *b* and *e*, *d* and *g*, *f* and *h*

2  *a* and *d* are not parallel to any of the other lines.

3  (a)  C     (b)  E     (c)  G
   (d)  O and possibly S

4  (a) and (b) The pupil's drawing
   (c)  The 'diamond' shape has its sides all the same length.
        Its opposite angles are the same size.
        Its two different angles add up to 180°.
        The diagonals cut one another in half, crossing at right angles.

5  (3, 4)

6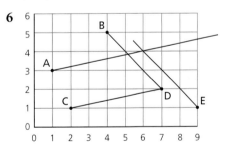

The cargo hold is at (6, 4).

# Review 1

1 (a) 1320     (b) 0545     (c) 2310

2 (a) 8:40 a.m.     (b) 3:25 p.m.
   (c) 10:05 a.m.

3 1 hour and 50 minutes

4 55 minutes

5 10:40 p.m.

6 (a) 25 minutes     (b) 37 minutes
   (c) 7 minutes

7 (a) $\frac{6}{8}$ or $\frac{3}{4}$   (b) $\frac{2}{6}$ or $\frac{1}{3}$   (c) $\frac{2}{4}$ or $\frac{1}{2}$

8 $\frac{3}{5}$

9 (a) $\frac{1}{2}$      (b) $\frac{1}{3}$      (c) $\frac{5}{6}$
   (d) $\frac{3}{4}$      (e) $\frac{7}{12}$

10 (a) $\frac{2}{8}$ or $\frac{1}{4}$     (b) $\frac{4}{8}$ or $\frac{1}{2}$

11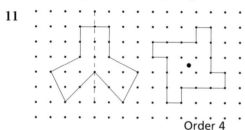
Order 4

12 (a) The pupil's copy of the shape with the centre of rotation marked at (5, 5).
   (b) 2
   (c) FE
   (d) AH and DE
   (e) The pupil's two right angles marked on the shape (∠BAH and ∠DEF are interior right angles, ∠BCD and ∠HGF are also right angles)

13 (a) 6      (b) 20      (c) 6
   (d) 12     (e) 15

14 (a) $\frac{4}{12}$ or $\frac{1}{3}$   (b) $\frac{5}{12}$     (c) 4

15 $\frac{2}{3}$

16 (a) Across '+5', down '+0'
   (b) Across '+2', down '−3'

17 (a)
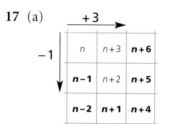

   (b)
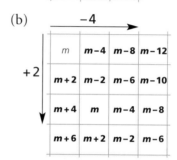

18 (a) $h + 7$    (b) $k + 3$    (c) $m - 7$
   (d) $2w + 4$    (e) $2n - 5$    (f) $3x - 3$

19 (a) and (b)
The coordinates of F are (12, 4).

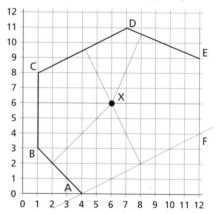

   (c) The route to CD is the shortest.

**Mixed questions 1** (Practice booklet p 25)

1  (a)  45 minutes or three-quarters of an
        hour

   (b)  35 minutes

   (c)  2 hours 35 minutes

   (d)  1 hour 25 minutes

2  (a)  9:05 a.m.      (b)  3:10 p.m.

   (c)  6:05           (d)  8:50 p.m.

3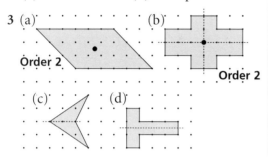

   (a) Order 2   (b) Order 2   (c)   (d)

4  (a)

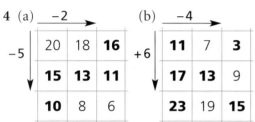

|       | −2 |    |    |
|-------|----|----|----|
| −5    | 20 | 18 | **16** |
|       | **15** | **13** | **11** |
|       | **10** | 8 | 6 |

   (b)

|       | −4 |    |    |
|-------|----|----|----|
| +6    | **11** | 7 | **3** |
|       | **17** | **13** | 9 |
|       | **23** | 19 | **15** |

   (c)

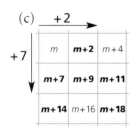

|       | +2 |      |        |
|-------|----|------|--------|
| +7    | *m* | *m*+2 | *m*+4 |
|       | *m*+7 | *m*+9 | *m*+11 |
|       | *m*+14 | *m*+16 | *m*+18 |

5  $\frac{1}{3}$

6  (a)  12   (b)  4   (c)  10   (d)  20

   (e)  6    (f)  12  (g)  8    (h)  16

   (i)  40   (j)  36  (k)  27   (l)  35

7  $\frac{1}{25}$ (or 0.04)

8  Lines *b* and *c* are parallel to one another
   (or they could be on the same line).

9  (a)  $\frac{3}{4}$ of 12 = 9    (b)  $\frac{3}{8}$ of 24 = 9

10  (a)  (i)  12     (ii)  6     (iii)  3

    (b)

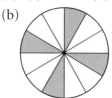

    (c)  (i)  12     (ii)  6     (iii)  3

# 8 Comparisons

This unit introduces median and range and uses these to compare sets of data. Pupils generate their own data in a reaction time experiment and use it to make comparisons. Other data handling projects are suggested and there is advice on writing up.

| **Essential** | **Optional** |
|---|---|
| Sheet 141 | Sheets 142 to 145 |
| **Practice booklet** pages 27 and 28 | |

## A Comparing heights (p 60)

◊ The discussion here is intended to be open, with no particular method of comparison preferred. The important thing is to give reasons for decisions.

  The two questions (about the picture and about the dot plots) can be given to pairs or small groups to consider before a general discussion.

  There may not always be a clear-cut answer.

◊ Pupils may suggest finding the mean. You could offer data where the mean of one group is greater than the mean of another, but only because of one extreme value (for example, 190, 150, 150, 150 and 159, 159, 159, 159). Work on the mean and discussion of which 'average' is more appropriate is dealt with later in the course.

## B  **Median** (p 62)

◊ You can introduce the median using the pupils' own heights. They will need to know their heights or will need to measure them.

Start by getting an odd number of pupils to stand in order of height. Emphasise that it is not the middle person who is the median of the group, but that person's height. It is a good idea to use 'median' only as an adjective at first, for example 'median height', 'median age'.

Then do the same with an even number of pupils.

To emphasise the value of the median as a way of comparing data, you may wish to carry out this activity with two separate groups (boys and girls or sides of the class).

## C  **Range** (p 64)

◊ The range can be shown practically with a group of pupils. Ask the group to stand in height order. Ask the tallest and shortest to stand side by side. Measure the difference between their heights.

## D  **How fast do you react?** (p 66)

Pupils work in pairs.

> Sheet 141

◊ In addition to comparing performance within each pair, pupils could compare left and right hands. For homework they could compare themselves with an adult.

◊ In one class pupils felt that they were getting clues from twitching fingers just before the ruler was dropped, so a card was used to cover the fingers.

◊ You may wish to work through section F (on report writing) first and get pupils to write up their work on reaction times. If so, you will need to explain the diagrams in section E as well.

## E  **Summarising data** (p 67)

The diagram in the pupil's book is a simplified version of the 'box and whisker' diagram, which shows the quartiles as well.

| Lowest | Lower quartile | Median | Upper quartile | Highest |

Either type of diagram may be arranged vertically.

Make sure pupils align the diagrams for each question correctly on a common scale, so that they can be used to make comparisons.

## F Writing a report (p 68)

The specimen report is intended to help pupils write their own reports. It can be used for either group or class discussion

◊ You may need to make it clear that the fastest person is the one with the shortest time, and vice versa.

## G Projects (p 70)

Each project generates data for making comparisons in a short written report.

### The Argon Factor

Sheets 142 and 143 (preferably on OHP transparencies), sheet 144

◊ There are two tests: mental agility and memory.

◊ In the mental agility test, give the pupils one minute to memorise the shapes and numbers on sheet 142. (They are best shown on an OHP.)

Tell pupils 'You will be given 5 seconds to answer each question. Questions will be read twice'.

1 What number is inside the circle?
2 What number is inside the pentagon?
3 What number is inside the first shape?
4 What shape has the number 17 in it?
5 What shape has the number 29 in it?
6 What number is inside the middle shape?
7 What number is inside the last shape?
8 What shape is in the middle?
9 What is the shape before the end one?
10 What number is in the second shape?
11 What shape is the one after the one with 21?
12 What number is inside the fourth shape?
13 What number is in the shape just right of the triangle?
14 What shape is two to the left of the kite?
15 What number is in the shape two after the circle?

'Argon factor is excellent as a class activity and well worth the time spent on it.'

◊ In the memory test, give the pupils two minutes to remember the pictures and details of the four people on sheet 143. (You might want to use fewer pictures or less information with some classes.)

Then give them ten minutes to write answers to the 20 questions on sheet 144.

◊ Discuss with the class what comparisons can be made from the scores. Suggestions include these.

- Do people remember more about their own sex?
- Which test did the class do better on? (Remember that the number of questions is not the same.)

**Other projects**

For 'Tile pattern' (see below), sheet 145

Another project idea is given on p 70 ('Handwriting size')

Another possibility is 'Tile pattern', for which sheet 145 is needed.
This is suitable for an individual pupil or a pair. The pupil(s) carrying out the project cut out the 16 tiles and put them in an envelope. They decide which groups of people are to be compared (for example, children and adults). Each 'subject' is then timed making the pattern shown on the sheet.

B **Median** (p 62)

**B1** (a) 159 cm  (b) 156 cm  (c) 154.5 cm

**B2** (a) 11  (b) 154 cm

**B3** A  Girls 136 cm; boys 153 cm
The boys are taller.

B  Girls 149.5 cm; boys 143 cm
The girls are generally taller.

C  Girls 143 cm; boys 149 cm
The boys are generally taller but the girls' heights are well spread out.

D  Girls 149 cm; boys 140 cm
The girls are generally taller but there are some short girls and one tall boy.

E  Girls 139 cm; boys 149 cm
The boys are generally taller but there is a tall girl and some short boys.

F  Girls 152 cm; boys 145 cm
The girls are generally taller.

**B4** (a) 152 cm  (b) 151 cm
(c) 153 cm  (d) 152.5 cm

**B5** (a) 69 kg  (b) No change
(c) No change  (d) Up by 1 kg

**B6** (a) 52, 54, 58, 60, 63, 65, 70
(b) 60 kg

**B7** (a) 152 cm (lengths in order are 139, 148, 152, 156, 161 cm)
(b) 36 kg (weights in order are 26, 29, 31, 34, 38, 39, 40, 45 kg)

**B8** Boys have the greater median weight (2.7 kg); the girls' median is 2.65 kg.

C **Range** (p 64)

**C1** (a) A 13 cm  B 11 cm  C 18 cm
(b) C  (c) B

**C2** (a) 13 minutes  (b) 4 minutes
(c) 9 minutes

**C3** (a) Herd B
(b) Herd A, because it has the greatest range
(c) Herd C, because it has the smallest range

**C4** (a) Median 28, range 12
(b) Median 85, range 29
(c) **Nicky** and **Carol** both had high scores, but **Nicky**'s scores were the more spread out of the two.
(d) Nicky's scores and **Martin**'s scores were both spread out, but **Nicky** had the higher scores of the two.

(e) **Paul** and **Martin** were both bad players because they had **low** median scores.

(f) Paul was a consistent player because the range of his scores was **low**.

**C5** (a) Northern: median 12 m, range 7 m
Southern: median 14.5 m, range 11m

(b) Southern trees are taller. Their heights are more spread out.

**C6** (a) Machine A: median 500 g, range 26 g
Machine B: median 498 g, range 5 g
Machine C: median 502 g, range 6 g
Machine D: median 514 g, range 25 g

(b) Machine B     (c) Machine D

(d) Machine C

(e) (Machine A) Inconsistent: it both underfilled and overfilled packs.

(f) Machine C. It usually put enough in a pack to avoid complaint without being too generous to the customer.

E **Summarising data** (p 67)

**E1** The pupil's diagrams

**E2** (a)(i) 10 ◄———Range 12———┼—► 22
Median 20

(ii) 6 ◄Range 8├————► 14
Median 10

(iii) 7 ◄————————┼—Range 17————► 24
Median 15

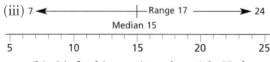

(b) Linford is consistently quick. He has the lowest median time and the smallest range.
Jules has some quick times, but is the least consistent, as shown by the large range.

**What progress have you made?** (p 70)

**1** Left hand: median 18, range 16
Right hand: median 14, range 6
Pat is faster and less variable using his right hand.

**Practice booklet**

**Sections A, B and C** (p 27)

**1** (a) 138 g     (b) 140     (c) 207

**2** (a)

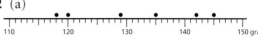

(b) 132 g

**3** (a) Barcelona 21°C   Birmingham 22°C

(b) Birmingham

(c) Barcelona  12 degrees
Birmingham  8 degrees

**Sections C and E** (p 28)

**1** The lengths are
A  27 mm    B  33 mm    C  36 mm
D  40 mm    E  56 mm    F  53 mm
Median length 38 mm
Range of lengths 26 mm

**2** (a) Median 85 kg, range 46 kg

(b) Median 7.8 m, range 3.3 m

(c) Median 1°C, range  10°C

(d) Median 37.7°C, range 2.8°C

**3** The pupil's comparison, such as
'The grey squirrels weigh more, because the median weight of the red squirrels is 293 g, and the median of the greys is 599 g. The greys are also more varied in weight, as the range of the reds is 25 g, but the range of the greys is 112 g.'

**4** On the whole, Jo is faster (the medians are 80.1 s and 81.7 s). Jo is also more consistent (the ranges are 3.4 s and 8.3 s). But Jay has had the fastest single run (76.2 s).

**5** Jo:
78.3 ◄—Range 3.4 ┼————► 81.7
Median 80.1

Jay:
76.2 ◄———Range 8.3 ┼———► 84.5
Median 81.7

# Hot and cold

This activity involves a lot of arithmetic and needs organisational skills.

Pupils imagine themselves to be running a stall selling ice creams and hot dogs. (In the simpler introductory version, there are only ice creams.) They get a forecast of tomorrow's temperature and have to decide how many ices and hot dogs to order. Then they find out the actual temperature, and how many of each they sell. (The forecast and actual temperatures are decided by the teacher throwing a dice.) Whatever isn't sold is wasted. The object, obviously, is to make as much profit as possible.

> Sheets 146 and 147 (one per pair)
> A dice

The activity is teacher-led, with pupils working in pairs, each pair running a stall.

◊ The simpler version, using sheet 146, is described here. The full version is similar, but with ice creams and hot dogs (sheet 147).

◊ Each pair starts with the same amount of money (for example £10). They record this in the Monday 'cash in box at start of day' cell.

◊ You throw the dice and announce the temperature forecast for Monday, as follows:

1 or 2: 10°C    3 or 4: 15°C    5 or 6: 20°C

◊ Each pair now has to decide how many ice creams (at 40p each) to order. Explain that the actual temperature could be above or below the forecast, as follows:

Forecast: 10°C    Actual will be 7°C or 12°C
Forecast: 15°C    Actual will be 12°C or 17°C
Forecast: 20°C    Actual will be 17°C or 22°C

The number sold will depend on the actual temperature:

7°C    0 sold        12°C    10 sold
17°C    15 sold        22°C    30 sold

When pupils have decided how many ices to order, they fill in the order on the sheet and work out the cash left in the box.

◊ Now you throw the dice again. If it lands odd, you go down from the forecast to get the actual temperature (for example, 15°C forecast becomes 12°C actual); if even, you go up.

◊ Each pair works out its sales, at 90p each. (They can't sell more than they ordered!) They work out the cash in their box at the end of the day. Then you start another round.

I tried this with top and bottom set. Both were hugely motivated and wanted to have several goes at it to improve their performances. We carried cash and supplies through week and worked out profits at end of week and had class winners'.

# 10 Inputs and outputs

This unit introduces pupils to equivalent expressions
such as $3(a + 6) = 3a + 18$ and $2(a - 4) = 2a - 8$.

In this unit, arrow diagrams are drawn with circles and ellipses. Pupils
may find it easier to use squares and rectangles in their diagrams.

> **Essential**
>
> Sheets 148 and 149
>
> **Practice booklet** pages 29 to 31

## Ⓐ Input and output diagrams (p 72)

**A5, A6**  These questions should get pupils thinking about looking for shorter
chains. By observing the number patterns (it may be helpful to add some
consecutive values to the table) they should be able to find shorter chains.

At the end of the unit, pupils could come back to these and try to prove
their results using algebra.

## Ⓑ Shorthand rules (p 74)

Pupils have met the fact that we can write $a \times 4$ as $4a$. Here the notation
is slightly extended, in that we write $(c + 5) \times 4$ as $4(c + 5)$. Revision of
'do what is in the brackets first' may be needed with some pupils.
The emphasis here is on using letters to write rules. However, pupils
consider numerical outputs in question B5.

◊ In discussing the notation, bring out the fact that any letter can be used to represent an input number, and that when multiplication is involved, the number comes first and the multiplication sign is omitted.

Mention that because $4 \times 3 = 3 \times 4$ we can (and do!) always put the number before the letter. You may want to use several examples like those in the introduction to ensure that pupils are secure with the notation. Include the fact that we can write $s \times 1$ as simply $s$.

◊ Ask pupils to choose some input numbers and find the outputs for the two diagrams at the top of page 74. They could think about whether for each input number the corresponding outputs are always different, and try this for different pairs of diagrams where the operations are swapped round.

## Ⓒ **Evaluating expressions** (p 76)

Sheet 148

◊ Your discussion should include how to use arrow diagrams to evaluate expressions with and without brackets. You could swap the operations in the example on the page to consider $5(p - 3)$.

◊ To break the ground for the 'Cover up' game, pupils could discuss different possible rules for a single input–output pair. For example, ask pupils in pairs to find as many rules as they can that fit $2 \rightarrow 5$.

## Ⓓ **Different rules?** (p 77)

This teacher-led section is for pupils to begin to consider when two rules are equivalent by looking at numerical examples.

◊ Pupils begin by matching each rule with an arrow diagram as they did in section C.

Now ask pupils to match each number pair in the bubble to as many of the rules as they can. They could record their results in tables:

| $n \rightarrow 2n + 10$ | $n \rightarrow n + 10$ | $n \rightarrow n + 1 + 9$ | $n \rightarrow 2(n + 5)$ |
|---|---|---|---|
| $10 \rightarrow 30$ | $1 \rightarrow 11$ | $1 \rightarrow 11$ | $10 \rightarrow 30$ |
| $3 \rightarrow 16$ | | | $3 \rightarrow 16$ |
| $2 \rightarrow 12$ | $2 \rightarrow 12$ | $2 \rightarrow 12$ | $2 \rightarrow 12 \ldots$ |

Pupils should notice that the lists for $n \rightarrow 2n + 10$ and $n \rightarrow 2(n + 5)$ are identical, as are the lists for the other pair of rules.

They are likely to be able to see that **any** input–output pair that fits $n \to n + 10$ will fit $n \to n + 1 + 9$ as the equivalence of 'add 10' and 'add 1 and then add 9' is familiar to them.

However, it is less obvious that **any** number pair that fits $n \to 2n + 10$ will fit $n \to 2(n + 5)$. The question of whether or not the two rules really are equivalent can be left unresolved till section E.

◊ In the second box, pupils copy and complete the table for each rule, perhaps drawing an arrow diagram for each rule first.

They should find that the rules seem to match up to give two equivalent pairs. Again the question of whether or not we really do have pairs of equivalent rules can be left unresolved till section E. Some pupils may be able to appreciate that agreement for some numerical examples does not in general give conclusive proof of equivalence.

## E **Equivalent expressions** (p 78)

This section follows on from the teacher-led section D. The initial discussion should include examples that involve subtraction.

Sheet 149 (one for each player)

◊ Diagrams such as the one on page 78 can help to explain why, for example, $3(n + 2) = (3 \times n) + (3 \times 2) = 3n + 6$.

You could also use simple areas to show the equivalence. For example:

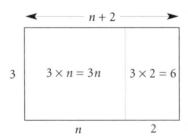

Include some examples where the number comes first in the brackets, for example $3(2 + n) = 6 + 3n$ or $3n + 6$.

◊ Discussion of numerical examples can help to explain the equivalence when the expression involves subtraction.

You could start by looking at addition and noticing, for example,
$3 \times (100 + 2) = (3 \times 100) + (3 \times 2) = 300 + 6 = 306$

Extend to subtraction:
$3 \times (100 - 2) = (3 \times 100) - (3 \times 2) = 300 - 6 = 294$

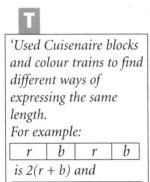

## Expression snap

◊ You may wish to copy the sets of cards on to different coloured card. If pairs of pupils have different coloured sets, it will help them sort the cards after each game.

### F Number tricks (p 79)

This extension material gives pupils the opportunity to use what they have learned to explain and create number puzzles where you always end up with the number first thought of.

### A Input and output machines (p 72)

**A1** (a) 3 (b) 12

**A2** (a) 13 (b) 16 (c) 1 (d) 37

**A3** (a)

$$17 \xrightarrow{\times 2} 34 \xrightarrow{-5} 29$$

(b)

$$6 \xrightarrow{\times 3} 18 \xrightarrow{-4} 14$$

(c)

$$12 \xrightarrow{+1} 13 \xrightarrow{\times 2} 26$$

(d)

$$2 \xrightarrow{\times 8} 16 \xrightarrow{+10} 26$$

**A4** (a) $2 \to 5$    (b) $6 \to 7$
$4 \to 11$        $16 \to 12$
$7 \to 20$        $0 \to 4$
$10 \to 29$      $3 \to 5\frac{1}{2}$

(c) $9 \to 21$    (d) $1 \to 11$
$4 \to 11$        $5 \to 31$
$5 \to 13$        $6 \to 36$
$7 \to 17$        $1\frac{1}{2} \to 13\frac{1}{2}$

*A5 (a) $2 \to 6$    (b) $1 \to 2$
$8 \to 24$        $5 \to 6$
$10 \to 30$      $39 \to 40$
$5 \to 15$        $9 \to 10$
$33 \to 99$      $7\frac{1}{2} \to 8\frac{1}{2}$
$0.5 \to 1.5$     $99 \to 100$

*A6 (a) $\bigcirc \xrightarrow{\times 3} \bigcirc$    (b) $\bigcirc \xrightarrow{+1} \bigcirc$

### B Shorthand rules (p 74)

**B1** (a)

$$b \xrightarrow{\times 3} 3b \xrightarrow{-2} 3b - 2$$

(b) $b \to 3b - 2$

**B2** (a)

$$p \xrightarrow{\times 3} 3p \xrightarrow{+4} 3p + 4$$

$p \to 3p + 4$

(b)

$$p \xrightarrow{+4} p + 4 \xrightarrow{\times 3} 3(p + 4)$$

$p \to 3(p + 4)$

**B3** Diagram C is correct.

$$s \xrightarrow{+2} s + 2 \xrightarrow{\times 3} 3(s + 2)$$

**B4** (a)

$$a \xrightarrow{\times 5} 5a \xrightarrow{-3} 5a - 3$$

$a \to 5a - 3$

(b)

$$a \xrightarrow{-3} a - 3 \xrightarrow{\times 5} 5(a - 3)$$

$a \to 5(a - 3)$

(c)

$$w \xrightarrow{+4} w + 4 \xrightarrow{\times 7} 7(w + 4)$$

$w \to 7(w + 4)$

(d)

$$w \xrightarrow{\times 7} 7w \xrightarrow{+4} 7w + 4$$

$w \to 7w + 4$

**B5** (a)

$$s \xrightarrow{\times 2} 2s \xrightarrow{+1} 2s+1$$

(b)

$$t \xrightarrow{-9} t-9 \xrightarrow{\times 3} 3(t-9)$$

(c)

$$w \xrightarrow{\times 5} 5w \xrightarrow{-7} 5w-7$$

(d)

$$x \xrightarrow{+7} x+7 \xrightarrow{\times 6} 6(x+7)$$

(e)

$$y \xrightarrow{\times 7} 7y \xrightarrow{+3} 7y+3$$

(f)

$$z \xrightarrow{+5} z+5 \xrightarrow{\times 2} 2(z+5)$$

When the input is 100, the outputs are

(a) 201    (b) 273    (c) 493
(d) 642    (e) 703    (f) 210

**B6** (a)

$$d \xrightarrow{+4} d+4 \xrightarrow{\times 3} \mathbf{3(d+4)}$$

$$d \to \mathbf{3(d-4)}$$

(b)

$$s \xrightarrow{\times 2} 2s \xrightarrow{+3} \mathbf{2s+3}$$

$$s \to \mathbf{3s+3}$$

(c)

$$g \xrightarrow{+1} g+1 \xrightarrow{\times 3} \mathbf{3(g+1)}$$

$$g \to \mathbf{3(g+1)}$$

(d)

$$a \xrightarrow{\times 3} \mathbf{3a} \xrightarrow{+1} \mathbf{3a+1}$$

$$a \to \mathbf{3a+1}$$

(e)

$$e \xrightarrow{\times 1} e \xrightarrow{+10} \mathbf{e+10}$$

$$e \to \mathbf{e+10}$$

(f)

$$j \xrightarrow{-3} j-3 \xrightarrow{\times 2} \mathbf{2(j-3)}$$

$$j \to \mathbf{2(j-3)}$$

ℂ **Evaluating expressions** (p 76)

**C1** 16

**C2** (a) 9    (b) 8    (c) 26    (d) 6

**C3** (a) 28    (b) 32    (c) 36    (d) 60

**C4** (a) $2 \to \mathbf{13}$    (b) $3 \to \mathbf{17}$
(c) $4 \to \mathbf{21}$    (d) $10 \to \mathbf{45}$

**C5** (a) $1 \to 4$
(b) $1 \to 4$ and $2 \to 9$
(c) $1 \to 4$ and $5 \to 12$
(d) $5 \to 0$
(e) $2 \to 9$
(f) $3 \to 0$ and $4 \to 5$

**C6** The pupil's three rules for $1 \to 6$

**Cover up**

One solution to board A is

| $p \to 5p-6$ | $a \to 5(a-2)$ |
|---|---|
| $t \to 3t$   $b \to 3b+4$    $x \to 2x+8$   $m \to m+6$ | |
| $w \to 3w-2$ | $y \to 3(y+2)$ |

A solution to board B is

| $w \to 3w-2$ | $p \to 5p-6$ | $b \to 3b+4$ |
|---|---|---|
| $y \to 3(y+2)$   $a \to 5(a-2)$ | $m \to m+6$ | |
| $t \to 3t$ | $x \to 2x+8$ | |

𝔼 **Equivalent expressions** (p 78)

**E1** $2(x+4)$ and $2x+8$
$2(x+8)$ and $2x+16$
$2(x+2)$ and $2x+4$
The odd one is $2(x+16)$.

**E2** $3a+18$ and $3(a+6)$
$3(a-2)$ and $3a-6$
$3a-18$ and $3(a-6)$
The odd one is $3a-2$.

**E3** (a) $3x + 15$ (b) $7b + 21$

(c) $5c + 20$ (d) $4d + 4$

(e) $12e + 24$ (f) $3w - 6$

(g) $4a - 12$ (h) $70m - 70$

(i) $12 + 6f$ or $6f + 12$

(j) $3y - 27$

(k) $40 + 8k$ or $8k + 40$

(l) $6n - 12$

**E4** (a) $2a + 10 = \mathbf{2}(a + 5)$

(b) $2(a - 6) = 2a - \mathbf{12}$

(c) $4a - 12 = 4(a - \mathbf{3})$

(d) $3(a + 7) = \mathbf{3}a + 21$

(e) $5a - 20 = \mathbf{5}(a - \mathbf{4})$

(f) $\mathbf{7}a + 14 = 7(a + \mathbf{2})$

(g) $2(\mathbf{6} + \mathbf{p}) = 12 + 2p$ or $2(\mathbf{p} + \mathbf{6}) = 12 + 2p$

(h) $4a - 32 = \mathbf{4}(a - \mathbf{8})$

F **Number tricks** (p 79)

*F1 (b) You get the number you started with each time.

(c) $n \to n + 2 \to \mathbf{5}(n + 2) = 5n + \mathbf{10}$ $\to \mathbf{5}n \to \mathbf{n}$

(d) The pupil's explanation, for example: 'You start with $n$ and end with $n$'.

*F2 Add **8**. Divide by **8**.

*F3 The pupil's instructions

**What progress have you made?** (p 80)

1

2 $3 \to \mathbf{11}$
$10 \to \mathbf{46}$
$5 \to \mathbf{21}$
$8 \to 36$

3 (a)

$a \to \mathbf{2a - 5}$

(b)

$s \to 4(s + 3)$

4

5 (a) 19 (b) 27 (c) 18 (d) 28

6 (a) $6 \to \mathbf{15}$ (b) $1 \to \mathbf{0}$

7 (a) $4x - 12$ (b) $5s + 5$

(c) $2b + 18$ (d) $6k - 24$

**Practice booklet**

**Sections A and B** (p 29)

1 (a)

(b)

2 (a) $1 \to \mathbf{1}$ (b) $2 \to \mathbf{45}$
$3 \to \mathbf{9}$ $4 \to \mathbf{63}$
$\mathbf{4} \to 13$ $\mathbf{1} \to 36$
$\mathbf{10} \to 37$ $\mathbf{7} \to 90$

(c) $1 \to \mathbf{4}$ (d) $2 \to \mathbf{14}$
$4 \to \mathbf{10}$ $5 \to \mathbf{32}$
$6 \to 14$ $\mathbf{3} \to 20$
$\mathbf{10} \to 22$ $\mathbf{0} \to 2$

(e) $8 \to \mathbf{29}$ (f) $1 \to \mathbf{4}$
$2 \to \mathbf{5}$ $3 \to \mathbf{6}$
$6 \to 21$ $7 \to 10$
$\mathbf{10} \to 37$ $\mathbf{0} \to 3$

3 (a)

$n \to 3n + 1$

(b)

$n \to 2(n + 5)$

(c)

$n \to 2n - 3$

(d)

$n \xrightarrow{-4} n-4 \xrightarrow{\times 5} 5(n-4)$

$n \rightarrow 5(n-4)$

(e)

$n \xrightarrow{+1} n+1 \xrightarrow{\times 10} 10(n+1)$

$n \rightarrow 10(n+1)$

(f)

$n \xrightarrow{\times 7} 7n \xrightarrow{-6} 7n-6$

$n \rightarrow 7n-6$

4 (a)

$p \xrightarrow{\times 2} 2p \xrightarrow{+3} 2p+3$

(b)

$m \xrightarrow{\times 2} 2m \xrightarrow{+6} 2m+6$

(c)

$x \xrightarrow{-3} x-3 \xrightarrow{\times 2} 2(x-3)$

(d)

$b \xrightarrow{\times 3} 3b \xrightarrow{+10} 3b+10$

(e)

$t \xrightarrow{+4} t+4 \xrightarrow{\times 3} 3(t+4)$

(f)

$n \xrightarrow{-1} n-1 \xrightarrow{\times 5} 5(n-1)$

When the input is 10, the outputs are

(a) 23    (b) 26    (c) 14

(d) 40    (e) 42    (f) 45

## Section C (p 30)

1 (a) 10   (b) 22   (c) 2   (d) 12

2 (a) 5   (b) 35   (c) 119 (d) 17

3 (a) $1 \rightarrow$ **18**     (b) $3 \rightarrow$ **24**

   (c) $10 \rightarrow$ **45**    (d) $100 \rightarrow$ **315**

4 $3(m+1)$ and $5(m+1)$ do not have the value 10, when $m = 3$.

5 (a) 49    (b) 37    (c) 3

   (d) 11    (e) 20    (f) 24

6 (a) 4    (b) 1    (c) 5

   (d) 1    (e) 3    (f) 1

## Section E (p 31)

1 $2(x+4) = 2x + 8$
$2(x+2) = 2x + 4$
$4(x+2) = 4x + 8$
$4(x+1) = 4x + 4$

2 $3(x-6) = 3x - 18$
$3(x-2) = 3x - 6$
$3(x-18) = 3x - 54$
$3(x-1) = 3x - 3$
Odd one out: $3x - 2$

3 (a) $2a + 6$      (b) $5x - 5$

   (c) $4p + 40$     (d) $10p + 40$

   (e) $7y + 21$     (f) $100c - 100$

   (g) $250 + 25t$ or $25t + 250$

   (h) $3n - 30$

   (i) $6 + 3j$ or $3j + 6$

4 (a) $2(x+3) = 2x + \mathbf{6}$

   (b) $\mathbf{4}(x+4) = 4x + 16$

   (c) $5x + 10 = \mathbf{5}(x + \mathbf{2})$

   (d) $2x - \mathbf{6} = \mathbf{2}(x-3)$

   (e) $3x + \mathbf{6} = \mathbf{3}(x+2)$

   (f) $\mathbf{4}(x+6) = 4x + 24$

# Fractions and decimals

Work on a limited range of decimals and fractions between 0 and 1 provides a visual approach to equivalence and comparing sizes.

As presented here, the work for the first four sections is largely based on a resource sheet. An alternative approach, which some teachers have found very successful, is outlined at the end of the notes for section A.

A decimal is of course a fraction, but in this unit the common use of 'decimal' to mean decimal fraction and 'fraction' to mean vulgar fraction is followed.

| **Essential** | **Optional** |
|---|---|
| Sheet 150 (preferably enlarged on to A3 paper) OHP transparency of sheet 150 | Centimetre squared paper, set squares and coloured pencils (for the alternative presentation) Sheet 151 (to make decimal fans) Various metric measuring rules and tapes |
| **Practice booklet** pages 32 to 37 | |

## A Putting fractions on a fraction ruler (p 81)

> Sheet 150, OHP transparency of sheet 150

◊ You could start by drawing a number line on the board and discussing where to label various points. Ask if pupils can label any points between 0 and 1, and explain that they will be zooming-in on the space between 0 and 1.

◊ On sheet 150, the space between 0 and 1 is represented by several scales, each divided into 100 equal parts. Check that pupils understand each division on this scale represents $\frac{1}{100}$. Ask pupils to label $\frac{10}{100}, \frac{20}{100}, \frac{30}{100} \cdots$ under the scale marked 'hundredths'. Pick out some other points such as $\frac{46}{100}, \frac{4}{100}$ and $\frac{35}{100}$, and ask pupils to mark them above the scale with arrows and label them.

Draw pupils' attention to the halves scale. How many halves can they label? Ask them to label $\frac{1}{2}$ below the scale. What is that in hundredths?

Repeat this with the quarters, fifths, twentieths and tenths scales.

◊ As the labelling proceeds you could start to ask pupils to compare the sizes of fractions on different scales and to say which are equivalent.

◊ You could ask pupils to suggest other fractions to mark on the blank scales at the bottom (twenty-fifths and fiftieths are the obvious ones).

## Alternative presentation

This approach is more time-consuming but teachers who have entered into the spirit of it have felt that pupils gained a greater sense of familiarity with the fractions.

One sheet of centimetre squared paper, about 30 cm by 120 cm, for every two pupils
Optional: Set square, coloured pencils

◊ Working in pairs, pupils first draw a line 100 cm long on the squared paper and label its ends 0 and 1. The larger format allows all of the hundredths to be labelled. Pupils can do this (perhaps working from opposite ends) in pencil first, so mistakes can be corrected.

Discuss the $\frac{50}{100}$ point and other ways it could be labelled. Decimals and percentages may arise as well as fractions. Now encourage pupils to think about other fractions they can mark. They should, for example, write $\frac{1}{4}$ below $\frac{25}{100}$, and put each 'family' of fractions (quarters, fifths and so on) on the same level. Colouring can help distinguish the families.

◊ Comparing the sizes of fractions and discussion of equivalence can then continue as with the resource sheet.

◊ Decimals can be added to the home-made fraction ruler as suggested in the guidance for section C.

## B Comparing fractions (p 81)

> Sheet 150

◊ The fraction ruler is meant to help pupils make sense of equivalence and comparisons but they should eventually become independent of it. So if you start this section with oral questioning, the emphasis should be on answering a question with the ruler visible and then trying to answer a similar one with it out of sight.

## C Putting decimals on the fraction ruler (p 83)

> Sheet 150, OHP transparency of sheet 150

◊ Remind pupils that another way of writing tenths is to use decimals. Ask them to label 0.1, 0.2, ... below the top scale. You can ask questions such as these (preferably with the fraction ruler now hidden) to check the basic idea is understood:

  • What decimal is halfway between 0 and 1?

  • How far is it between 0.2 and 0.6 as a decimal (and as a fraction)?

◊ Explain that decimals can also be used to write hundredths; for example, $\frac{46}{100}$ is 0.46. Ask pupils to mark these with arrows above the decimals scale and label them: 0.14, 0.36, 0.45, 0.78, ... When they are confident about this ask them to label 0.10, 0.20, 0.30, ... above the decimals scale.

◊ Referring to the fraction ruler, draw pupils' attention to the equivalences $0.50 = \frac{50}{100} = \frac{5}{10} = 0.5$. They can write their own sets of equivalences for 0.40 and so on.

◊ Ask how they should write $\frac{3}{100}$ as a decimal. If anyone says 0.3 (a common error), rather than saying this is wrong you could ask them what $\frac{30}{100}$ is as a decimal. Reflecting back a mistaken answer like this so that pupils have to sort out the resulting conflict often works better than simply telling them what is right and wrong. Make sure 0.03 is now correctly marked above the decimals scale.

Similarly, point to the mark halfway between 0 and 0.1 on the decimal scale and ask pupils to write it down as a decimal. If any write 0.5 ask them whether 0.5 is marked anywhere else on the sheet.

◊ To build confidence with two places of decimals, ask questions like

  • What number is halfway between 0.8 and 0.9?

  • How far is it from 0.34 to 0.4?

The emphasis should be on using the sheet for support then trying to answer similar questions without the sheet in sight.

◊ Also ask questions like
  • Which is bigger, 0.39 or 0.7? (common error 0.39)
  • Which is bigger, 0.09 or 0.2? (common error 0.09)
Here too, try a reflecting-back approach when errors occur.

## D Decimals and fractions (p 83)

> Optional: Decimal fans made from sheet 151

Again, the aim is to make pupils independent of the sheet once it has
served to build their confidence and understanding.

◊ The decimal fan (made by cutting out the pieces on sheet 151, piercing
where marked and holding together with a brass fastener) is designed to
promote instant recall of decimal equivalents. Pupils can each have a fan
and you can ask (for example) 'Make a decimal equal to $\frac{4}{5}$'; pupils all
show what they have made and you can soon see if anyone is having
difficulty. Or you can make different decimals on two fans, hold them up
to the class and ask which is bigger.

Less confident pupils have found it easier to use a fan made from just the
left-hand set of cards on the resource sheet (0 to 9 and the decimal
point).

## E Mixed numbers (p 86)

## F Up to two decimal places (p 86)

Relationships between tenths, hundredths and decimals, already explored
in the fraction ruler work, are now extended to numbers greater than 1.
All calculations are meant to be done without a calculator.

**F10** Here, and in other similar questions, the aim is to get pupils thinking
about place value in the numbers they are working with. They should not
need to set the calculations out in columns.

## G Decimals of a metre (p 89)

Decimals of a metre are related to metres and centimetres.

**G13** It is well worth supplementing this with measurement of classroom
objects using differently marked tapes and rulers.

## B Comparing fractions (p 81)

Answers given here are those available from the fraction ruler. Other correct answers may be possible.

**B1** $\frac{10}{100}$, $\frac{2}{20}$

**B2** (a) $\frac{25}{100}$ or $\frac{5}{20}$  (b) $\frac{6}{10}$, $\frac{60}{100}$ or $\frac{12}{20}$

   (c) $\frac{75}{100}$ or $\frac{3}{4}$  (d) $\frac{13}{20}$

**B3** $\frac{4}{5}$

**B4** $\frac{1}{20}$, $\frac{1}{2}$, $\frac{3}{5}$, $\frac{7}{10}$

**B5** 4

**B6** (a) $\frac{2}{5} = \frac{\mathbf{8}}{20}$  (b) $\frac{\mathbf{3}}{\mathbf{5}} = \frac{12}{20}$

   (c) $\frac{4}{5} = \frac{\mathbf{16}}{20}$  (d) $\frac{1}{5} = \frac{\mathbf{4}}{20}$

**B7** 5

**B8** (a) $\frac{7}{20} = \frac{\mathbf{35}}{100}$  (b) $\frac{\mathbf{3}}{\mathbf{20}} = \frac{15}{100}$

   (c) $\frac{4}{20} = \frac{\mathbf{20}}{100}$  (d) $\frac{11}{20} = \frac{\mathbf{55}}{100}$

**B9** (a) $\frac{1}{2} = \frac{\mathbf{10}}{20}$  (b) $\frac{3}{5} = \frac{\mathbf{6}}{10}$

   (c) $\frac{\mathbf{4}}{\mathbf{10}} = \frac{8}{20}$  (d) $\frac{7}{10} = \frac{\mathbf{70}}{100}$

   (e) $\frac{3}{4} = \frac{15}{\mathbf{20}}$  (f) $\frac{30}{100} = \frac{6}{\mathbf{20}}$

   (g) $\frac{18}{20} = \frac{90}{\mathbf{100}}$  (h) $\frac{3}{5} = \frac{60}{100}$

**B10** (a) $\frac{55}{100}$  (b) $\frac{3}{20}$  (c) $\frac{19}{50}$  (d) $\frac{1}{25}$

**B11** $\frac{2}{5} = \frac{8}{20}$, $\frac{1}{4} = \frac{5}{20}$ so $\frac{2}{5}$ is bigger.

**B12** Three fractions from $\frac{5}{10}$, $\frac{50}{100}$, $\frac{2}{4}$, $\frac{10}{20}$

**B13** (a) $\frac{75}{100}$ or $\frac{15}{20}$  (b) $\frac{4}{10}$ or $\frac{40}{100}$ or $\frac{8}{20}$

   (c) $\frac{25}{100}$ or $\frac{1}{4}$  (d) $\frac{3}{10}$ or $\frac{6}{20}$

**B14** $\frac{1}{2}$

**B15** $\frac{20}{100}$, $\frac{3}{4}$, $\frac{9}{10}$

**B16** 2

**B17** (a) $\frac{2}{10} = \frac{\mathbf{4}}{20}$  (b) $\frac{\mathbf{6}}{\mathbf{10}} = \frac{12}{20}$

   (c) $\frac{7}{10} = \frac{\mathbf{14}}{20}$  (d) $\frac{9}{10} = \frac{\mathbf{18}}{20}$

**B18** (a) $\frac{1}{2} = \frac{\mathbf{2}}{4}$  (b) $\frac{1}{5} = \frac{\mathbf{2}}{10}$  (c) $\frac{2}{5} = \frac{\mathbf{8}}{20}$

   (d) $\frac{2}{10} = \frac{\mathbf{20}}{100}$  (e) $\frac{1}{2} = \frac{5}{\mathbf{10}}$  (f) $\frac{1}{4} = \frac{5}{\mathbf{20}}$

   (g) $\frac{2}{5} = \frac{4}{\mathbf{10}}$  (h) $\frac{15}{100} = \frac{3}{\mathbf{20}}$

## D Decimals and fractions (p 83)

Answers given here are those available from the fraction ruler. Other correct answers may be possible.

**D1** The pupil's labelled arrows on the decimals scale

**D2** Marked on the decimals scale:

   (a) 0.85  (b) 0.15  (c) 0.75

**D3** (a) 0.35  (b) 0.25  (c) 0.55

**D4** Two fractions from each of these:

   (a) $\frac{8}{10}$, $\frac{80}{100}$, $\frac{4}{5}$, $\frac{16}{20}$  (b) $\frac{55}{100}$, $\frac{11}{20}$

   (c) $\frac{15}{100}$, $\frac{3}{20}$  (d) $\frac{9}{10}$, $\frac{90}{100}$, $\frac{18}{20}$

**D5** (a) 0.6  (b) 0.9  (c) 0.2  (d) 0.7

**D6** 2

**D7** (a) 0.6  (b) 0.2  (c) 0.4  (d) 0.8

**D8** (a) 0.8  (b) 0.35  (c) 0.48  (d) 0.09

**D9** 0.05, 0.45, 0.5, 0.54, 0.6

**D10** (a) $\frac{35}{100}$, 0.35  (b) $\frac{5}{100}$, 0.05

   (c) $\frac{45}{100}$, 0.45  (d) $\frac{55}{100}$, 0.55

**D11** (a) 0.1  (b) 0.95  (c) 0.9  (d) 0.3

   (e) 0.92  (f) 0.2  (g) 0.75  (h) 0.07

**D12** (a) $\frac{47}{100}$  (b) $\frac{99}{100}$  (c) $\frac{2}{100}$  (d) $\frac{77}{100}$

**D13** 0.04, 0.12, $\frac{1}{2}$, 0.7

**D14** 0.09, $\frac{62}{100}$, 0.71, $\frac{3}{4}$, 0.8

**D15** (a) 0.77  (b) 0.79  (c) $\frac{4}{5}$

**D16** He is not correct. 0.28 is $\frac{28}{100}$, 0.7 is $\frac{7}{10}$. So you cannot just compare the 28 and the 7 (or a similar explanation).

**D17** 2

**D18** (a) $\frac{6}{100}$, 0.06  (b) $\frac{98}{100}$, 0.98

   (c) $\frac{34}{100}$, 0.34  (d) $\frac{66}{100}$, 0.66

**D19** 4

**D20** (a) $\frac{44}{100}$, 0.44    (b) $\frac{8}{100}$, 0.08

     (c) $\frac{96}{100}$, 0.96    (d) $\frac{76}{100}$, 0.76

**D21** (a) 0.65    (b) 0.45    (c) 0.95

**D22** (a) 0.7   (b) 0.65   (c) 0.6   (d) 0.25

**D23** (a) $\frac{92}{100}$   (b) $\frac{43}{100}$   (c) $\frac{29}{100}$   (d) $\frac{61}{100}$

**D24** Two fractions from each of these:
     (a) $\frac{6}{10}, \frac{60}{100}, \frac{3}{5}, \frac{12}{20}$    (b) $\frac{5}{10}, \frac{50}{100}, \frac{1}{2}, \frac{2}{4}, \frac{10}{20}$
     (c) $\frac{75}{100}, \frac{3}{4}, \frac{15}{20}$    (d) $\frac{45}{100}, \frac{9}{20}$

**D25** 0.08, 0.34, 0.6, 0.91

**D26** (a) Fifths      (b) $\frac{3}{5}$

     (c) Twentieths    (d) $\frac{13}{20}$

     (e) Quarters      (f) $\frac{3}{4}$

### E Mixed numbers (p 86)

**E1** (a) 2.75 (b) 1.6   (c) 5.9   (d) 10.5

**E2** (a) $8\frac{1}{4}$   (b) $7\frac{1}{5}$   (c) $9\frac{2}{5}$   (d) $3\frac{17}{20}$
     (Other equivalent fractions are possible.)

**E3** $2\frac{1}{5}$, $2\frac{1}{4}$, $2\frac{13}{20}$, $2\frac{3}{4}$, $2\frac{9}{10}$

**E4** There are 4 quarters in 1.
     So there are 8 quarters in 2.
     The extra quarter makes 9 quarters.

**E5** (a) 16    (b) 23    (c) 51    (d) 44

**E6** (a) $1\frac{3}{5}$      (b) $1\frac{1}{3}$      (c) $1\frac{1}{5}$
     (d) $2\frac{1}{4}$      (e) $2\frac{1}{10}$

**E7** (a) $5 \times \frac{3}{4} = \frac{15}{4}$    (b) $4 \times \frac{4}{5} = \frac{16}{5}$
     (c) $9 \times \frac{7}{10} = \frac{63}{10}$    (d) $5 \times \frac{5}{8} = \frac{25}{8}$

**E8** (a) $3\frac{3}{4}$   (b) $3\frac{1}{5}$   (c) $6\frac{3}{10}$   (d) $3\frac{1}{8}$

**E9** (a) $2\frac{2}{5}$      (b) $7\frac{1}{3}$      (c) $4\frac{4}{5}$
     (d) $2\frac{5}{8}$      (e) $8\frac{1}{10}$

### F Up to two decimal places (p 86)

**F1** (a) 2.64 cm   (b) 2.18 cm

**F2** (a) 6.23      (b) 6.37      (c) 6.42
     (d) 6.47      (e) 6.51      (f) 6.58

**F3** (a) 8.25      (b) 4.95      (c) 2.45
     (d) 6.05      (b) 3.85      (f) 10.05

**F4** 2.35 and 2.4

**F5** 5.17, 5.03 and 5.1

**F6** (a) 5.09, 5.32, 5.76, 5.84, 6
     (b) 2.8, 3.07, 3.19, 3.2, 3.5
     (c) 0.15, 0.45, 0.6, 1.07, 1.1

**F7** HOLIDAYS

**F8** ENJOYABLE

**F9** (a) 7 hundreds or 700
     (b) 2 thousands or 2000
     (c) 3 units or 3
     (d) 1 ten or 10
     (e) 8 hundredths or 0.08

**F10** (a) 2723.58      (b) 3713.58
     (c) 2713.68      (d) 2714.58
     (e) 2713.59      (e) 2813.58

**F11** (a) 7 tenths      (b) 3 hundredths
     (c) 6 tens      (d) 8 tenths
     (e) 4 hundredths (f) 5 tenths

**F12** (a) 46.6      (b) 55.6      (c) 45.7
     (d) 7.44      (e) 7.35      (f) 8.34
     (g) 29.74      (h) 28.84      (i) 28.75

**F13** 60

**F14** 0.7

**F15** 0.03

**F16** 5 units + 5 tenths + 8 hundredths
     or 5 units + 58 hundredths
     or 558 hundredths
     (possibly also 55 tenths + 8 hundredths)

**F17** 1 unit + 8 hundredths
     or 108 hundredths
     (possibly also 10 tenths + 8 hundredths)

**F18** 7 units + 5 tenths + 1 hundredth
or 7 units + 51 hundredths
or 751 hundredths
(possibly also 75 tenths + 1 hundredth)

**F19** 4 tenths + 2 hundredths or
42 hundredths

**F20** (a) 4.84 (b) 9.01 (c) 0.79 (d) 2.26

### Ⓖ Decimals of a metre (p 89)

**G1** (a) 6.75 m (b) 5.32 m (c) 2.04 m
(d) 10.11 m (e) 8.20 m or 8.2 m

**G2** (a) 2.48 m (b) 5.03 m
(c) 0.22 m (d) 6.30 m or 6.3 m

**G3** (a) 1 metre and 98 centimetres
(b) 4 metres and 6 centimetres
(c) 9 metres and 80 centimetres
(d) 10 metres and 10 centimetres

**G4** (a) 6 metres and 22 centimetres
(b) 3 metres and 30 centimetres
(c) 10 metres and 1 centimetre
(d) 4 metres and 8 centimetres

**G5** (a) 40 cm (b) 820 cm
(c) 705 cm (d) 5 cm

**G6** 2.09 m, 2.11 m, 232 cm, 2.4 m

**G7** 0.07 m, 0.32 m, 40 cm, 0.5 m

**G8** (a) 4.2 m (b) Barker's
(b) Church's (b) 4.5 m

**G9** 4.12 m

**G10** 30 centimetres

**G11** 1.67 m

**G12** 18 centimetres

**G13** (a) 3.82 m (b) 3.88 m
(c) 3.90 m or 3.9 m
(d) 3.94 m (e) 1.25 m
(f) 1.30 m or 1.3 m
(g) 1.38 m (h) 1.41 m
(i) 2.91 m (j) 2.96 m
(k) 3.01 m (l) 3.05 m
(m) 0.99 m (n) 1.01 m
(o) 1.05 m (p) 1.09 m
(q) 1.13 m

### What progress have you made? (p 91)

**1** For each part, one of the fractions given,
or another equivalent fraction:
(a) $\frac{2}{10}, \frac{20}{100}, \frac{1}{4}$ (b) $\frac{3}{10}, \frac{30}{100}$
(c) $\frac{9}{20}$ (d) $\frac{80}{100}, \frac{4}{5}, \frac{16}{20}$

**2** $\frac{3}{4}$

**3** $\frac{1}{2}, \frac{3}{5}, \frac{7}{10}, \frac{15}{20}$

**4** (a) $\frac{4}{10}$ (b) $\frac{7}{20}$ (c) $\frac{71}{100}$ (d) $\frac{3}{100}$
(or other equivalent fractions)

**5** (a) 0.4 (b) 0.15
(c) 0.09 (d) 0.14

**6** (a) 3.4 (b) 10.25
(c) 9.9 (d) 1.05

**7** (a) $4\frac{1}{5}$ (b) $9\frac{3}{4}$ (c) $3\frac{1}{20}$ (d) $4\frac{11}{20}$
(or other equivalent fractions)

**8** (a) 6.99 (b) 7.09
(c) 7.15 (d) 7.2 or 7.20
(e) 7.24

**9** (a) 7.92 (b) 4.27 (c) 7.92 (d) 22.92

**10** 2.32 m

## Practice booklet

### Section B (p 32)

In questions 2, 3 and 4 other equivalent fractions are possible.

1  $\frac{30}{100}$, $\frac{6}{20}$ and $\frac{3}{10}$

2  $\frac{8}{10}$, $\frac{16}{20}$ or $\frac{80}{100}$

3  $\frac{1}{2}$, $\frac{5}{10}$ or $\frac{50}{100}$

4  (a)  $\frac{14}{20}$ or $\frac{70}{100}$       (b)  $\frac{3}{4}$ or $\frac{75}{100}$

   (c)  $\frac{11}{20}$                      (d)  $\frac{35}{100}$

5  5

6  (a)  $\frac{4}{5} = \frac{20}{25}$       (b)  $\frac{15}{25} = \frac{3}{5}$

   (c)  $\frac{1}{5} = \frac{\mathbf{5}}{25}$       (d)  $\frac{10}{25} = \frac{\mathbf{2}}{5}$

7  2

8  (a)  $\frac{\mathbf{74}}{100} = \frac{37}{50}$       (b)  $\frac{\mathbf{42}}{50} = \frac{84}{100}$

   (c)  $\frac{4}{100} = \frac{\mathbf{2}}{50}$       (d)  $\frac{19}{50} = \frac{\mathbf{38}}{100}$

9  (a)  $\frac{2}{10}$, $\frac{2}{5}$, $\frac{2}{4}$

   (b)  $\frac{5}{10}$, $\frac{3}{4}$, $\frac{4}{5}$

   (c)  $\frac{3}{5}$, $\frac{73}{100}$, $\frac{19}{20}$

10  (a)  $\frac{17}{20} = \frac{\mathbf{85}}{100}$  (b)  $\frac{3}{4} = \frac{15}{\mathbf{20}}$  (c)  $\frac{4}{5} = \frac{16}{\mathbf{20}}$

   (d)  $\frac{1}{5} = \frac{20}{\mathbf{100}}$  (e)  $\frac{42}{50} = \frac{21}{\mathbf{25}}$  (f)  $\frac{16}{25} = \frac{\mathbf{64}}{100}$

   (g)  $\frac{7}{10} = \frac{35}{\mathbf{50}}$  (h)  $\frac{1}{2} = \frac{25}{\mathbf{50}}$

11  (a)  $\frac{3}{4}$   (b)  $\frac{9}{20}$   (c)  $\frac{15}{20}$   (d)  $\frac{4}{10}$

### Section D (p 33)

1  Two fractions from each of these (or other equivalent fractions)

   (a)  $\frac{3}{5}$, $\frac{6}{10}$, $\frac{12}{20}$, $\frac{60}{100}$

   (b)  $\frac{9}{20}$, $\frac{45}{100}$

   (c)  $\frac{19}{20}$, $\frac{95}{100}$

   (d)  $\frac{1}{5}$, $\frac{2}{10}$, $\frac{4}{20}$, $\frac{20}{100}$

2  (a)  0.5  (b)  0.7  (c)  0.6  (d)  0.25

3  (a)  0.38  (b)  0.03  (c)  0.85  (d)  0.16

4  (a)  0.14, 0.22, $\frac{1}{4}$, 0.3

   (b)  $\frac{12}{25}$, 0.56, $\frac{73}{100}$, 0.8

   (c)  0.08, $\frac{34}{100}$, 0.49, 0.6, $\frac{3}{4}$

   (d)  0.04, 0.28, $\frac{30}{100}$, 0.32, $\frac{9}{20}$

5  (a)  0.43       (b)  0.41       (c)  0.55

### Section E (p 33)

1  (a)  2.9  (b)  1.5  (c)  6.4  (d)  11.25

2  (a)  $8\frac{2}{5}$  (b)  $4\frac{1}{4}$  (c)  $1\frac{13}{20}$  (d)  $7\frac{3}{10}$
   or other equivalent fractions

3  $2\frac{4}{5}$, $2\frac{9}{10}$, $3\frac{3}{20}$, $3\frac{19}{100}$, $3\frac{1}{4}$

4  (a)  $2\frac{3}{4}$  (b)  $4\frac{2}{5}$  (c)  $6\frac{3}{10}$

### Section F (p 34)

1  (a)  3.94  (b)  3.99  (c)  4.02  (d)  4.07
   (e)  4.15  (f)  4.22  (g)  4.26  (h)  4.31

2  (a)  2.07, 2.39, 2.5, 2.8

   (b)  1.01, 1.1, 1.43, 1.5

   (c)  4.09, 4.24, 4.25, 4.3, 5

   (d)  0.08, 0.65, 0.7, 1, 1.5

3  6.17, 6.3 and 6.37

4  TRIANGLE

5  6.06 or 6.48

6  (a)  7 hundreds or 700

   (b)  3 tenths or 0.3

   (c)  1 unit or 1

   (d)  9 hundredths or 0.09

7  (a)  63.7       (b)  72.7       (c)  62.9

   (d)  38.74       (e)  33.74       (f)  39.64

   (g)  39.73       (h)  30.1       (i)  30

8 (a) $458.1 + \mathbf{10} = 468.1$

  (b) $34.91 + \mathbf{0.01} = 34.92$

  (c) $103.6 + \mathbf{50} = 153.6$

  (d) $75.32 - \mathbf{1} = 74.32$

  (e) $54.8 - \mathbf{0.8} = 54$

  (f) $587.5 + \mathbf{400} = 987.5$

  (g) $6.77 - \mathbf{0.7} = 6.07$

  (h) $6.77 - \mathbf{0.07} = 6.7$

  (i) $204.2 - \mathbf{4} = 200.2$

9 266.24

10 150.46

11 227.38

12 (a) 0.68     (b) 3.71

  (c) 4.40 or 4.4   (d) 4.01

  (e) 5.8     (f) 10.06

## Section G (p 36)

1 (a) 3.27 m  (b) 7.83 m  (c) 1.56 m

  (d) 5.64 m  (e) 4.98 m  (f) 2.09 m

2 A and H, B and D, C and G, E and F

3 (a) 2.09 m

  (b) 3.2 m or 3.20 m

  (c) 4.8 m or 4.80 m

  (d) 9.01 m

  (e) 6.4 m or 6.40 m

  (f) 6.04 m

4

| Name | Height in cm | Height in metres and cm | Height in metres |
|---|---|---|---|
| Mel | 152 cm | **1 m 52 cm** | **1.52 m** |
| Ginger | **149 cm** | 1 m 49 cm | **1.49 m** |
| Ali | **159 cm** | **1 m 59 cm** | 1.59 m |
| Kay | **109 cm** | 1 m 9 cm | **1.09 m** |
| Morag | **160 cm** | **1 m 60 cm** | 1.60 m |

5 (a) Toni

  (b) Jamie, Geri, Suki, Paul, Toni

6 2.87 m, 2.9 m, 3.08 m, 3.1 m

7 0.05 m, 0.5 m, 0.9 m, 1.01 m

8 B and C

9 (a) 2.32 m  (b) 2.35 m  (c) 2.37 m

  (d) 2.41 m  (e) 5.01 m  (f) 5.06 m

  (g) 5.1 m or 5.10 m     (h) 5.12 m

**Investigations**

Investigative and problem-solving work are best integrated into the
development of mathematical concepts and skills. However, focusing
on investigative work, as here, allows important skills of report writing
to be developed. It is not intended that all the investigations should be
done together or in the order given.

| Essential | Optional |
|---|---|
| Counters, tiles or pieces of paper (for B3) | Counters, tiles or pieces of paper (for B1) |
| | Square dotty paper (for B6) |

## Ⓐ Crossing points (p 92)

Discussion of the report is intended to highlight some important
processes, for example, specialising, tabulating, generalising, predicting,
checking, explaining, drawing conclusions. It is not intended to suggest
there is one 'correct' way to approach an investigation and write up the
findings.

◊ If pupils find it difficult to follow Chris's written work, try to involve
them actively. They could read through the first half of page 93 (the 1, 2
and 3 line results) and then try with 4 lines.
Emphasise that the lines should be drawn as long as possible so that all
crossings are shown.

Ask pupils to find as many different numbers of crossings as possible
with 4 lines; 0, 1, 3, 4, 5 and 6 are possible:

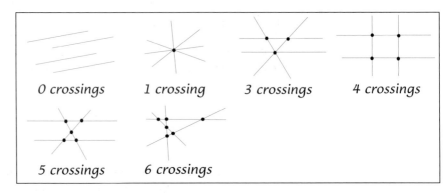

| 0 crossings | 1 crossing | 3 crossings | 4 crossings |

| 5 crossings | 6 crossings |

Ask how we can be sure that 2 crossings cannot be achieved or that 6 is
the maximum number. Emphasise that pupils should try to explain their
findings wherever possible.

◊ Now discuss how the investigation could proceed. Looking at the maximum number of crossing points is one choice (and it's the one made by the pupil in the write-up). Look at the results in the table. Pupils could try to spot a pattern before turning to page 95.

◊ Look at the table on page 95 and ask pupils if they can explain why the numbers of crossing points go up in the way they do. This is easier when pupils have found these results out for themselves. To get the maximum number of crossing points each additional line needs to cross all the lines in the diagram (except itself). Chris does not try to explain this in her report but without it she cannot be sure that the sequence of numbers continues in the way she describes. Point out that 'predict and check' may help to confirm results but is not foolproof (suppose there were actually 16 crossing points for 6 lines and your 'pattern' stopped you looking any further than 15).

◊ You could ask what the maximum number of crossing points would be with, say, 100 lines. Using Chris's method, this would take some time. With $n$ lines, each line crosses $n-1$ lines to produce $n-1$ crossing points. However, $n(n-1)$ counts each crossing point twice so the number of crossing points is $\frac{n(n-1)}{2}$.

◊ As a further investigation, pupils can look at the maximum number of closed regions obtained. An interesting result is that you get the same set of numbers but with 0 included: 0, 1, 3, 6, 10, 15, …

## Ⓑ **Some ideas**

### **B1 Round table** (p 96)

> Optional: Counters, tiles or pieces of paper may be useful to represent the people round the table.

◊ Pupils may find it helpful to do the investigation by moving counters or tiles (labelled A to E) round a drawing of a table. There is only one other arrangement:

Ask pupils to consider how they know there are no other arrangements. They may realise that every person has sat next to every other person so no other arrangements are possible. Ask pupils if that is what they expected – often pupils think there will be more possibilities.

◊ In one school, the investigation proved easier when the table was 'unrolled' into a straight line (remembering that the two end people are in fact sitting next to each other). For five people the two different arrangements are

ABCDE          ADBEC

◊ The results for 3 to 10 people are

| Number of people | Numbers of arrangements |
|:---:|:---:|
| 3 | 1 |
| 4 | 1 |
| 5 | 2 |
| 6 | 2 |
| 7 | 3 |
| 8 | 3 |
| 9 | 4 |
| 10 | 4 |

For an even number of people the rule is $a = \frac{p-2}{2}$
and for an odd number of people the rule is $a = \frac{p-1}{2}$
where $a$ is the number of arrangements
and $p$ is the number of people.

Since each person has two neighbours, the number of arrangements has to be the number of complete pairs of people that can sit next to an individual. These formulas give the number of complete pairs.

Very few pupils are likely to express the results algebraically at this stage.

## B2 Nine lines (p 96)

◊ Clarify that the grids of squares have to be drawn with straight lines either parallel to each other or at right angles.

As in *Crossing points* lines should be drawn as long as possible so that all possible squares are counted. For example, diagrams such as this are not considered valid.

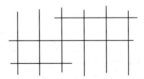

◊ With 9 lines 0, 6, 10 and 12 squares are possible:

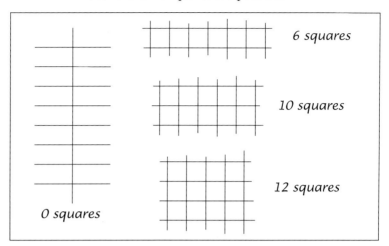

6 squares

10 squares

12 squares

0 squares

9 parallel lines will also produce 0 squares.

◊ All possible numbers of squares for 4 to 12 lines are

| Number of lines | Numbers of squares |
|---|---|
| 4 | 0  1 |
| 5 | 0  2 |
| 6 | 0  3  4 |
| 7 | 0  4  6 |
| 8 | 0  5  8  9 |
| 9 | 0  6  10  12 |
| 10 | 0  7  12  15  16 |
| 11 | 0  8  14  18  20 |
| 12 | 0  9  16  21  24  25 |

Pupils who produce a full set of results as in the table may make various observations such as:

• The minimum is always 0 and this can be achieved by a set of parallel lines.

• The next possible number of squares is $n - 3$ for $n$ lines. These numbers go up by 1 each time.

◊ Encourage pupils to follow their own lines of investigation. For example, they could consider the maximum number of squares possible each time.

Encourage pupils to describe how the lines should be arranged to give the maximum number of squares by asking questions such as 'How would you arrange 100 lines to achieve the maximum number of squares?' and 'What about 99 lines?'

Formulas are

even numbers of lines: $s = (\frac{n}{2} - 1)^2$

odd numbers of lines: $s = (\frac{n}{2} - \frac{1}{2})(\frac{n}{2} - \frac{3}{2})$

Again, very few pupils are likely to express their conclusions algebraically at this stage.

### B3 Swapover (p 97)

> Counters, tiles or pieces of paper

◊ It is useful for pupils to draw large grids so the counters have plenty of room to move, especially diagonally.

◊ You may need to emphasise the starting position with the empty space on the right. The following starting position is not valid:

*'Some found it frustrating at first. It helped if pupils worked in small groups.'*

◊ Once pupils think they have found a solution to the puzzle on the page and are confident they can repeat it, they could think about ways of recording their results. Some will want to draw a diagram for each move. Encourage more able pupils to find efficient ways of presenting their results.

◊ Most pupils will tend to move the counters horizontally and vertically to start with. You may need to remind them they can move diagonally.

◊ 7 is the least number of moves for the grid shown.
The moves are

The method for the least number of moves can be described as always to move counters diagonally to the opposite side except where impossible. It can be easier to see this on larger grids.

◊ The minimum number of moves for various sizes of grid are

| Counters in one line | Number of moves |
|---|---|
| 1 | 3 |
| 2 | 5 |
| 3 | 7 |
| 4 | 9 |
| 5 | 11 |
| 6 | 13 |
| 7 | 15 |
| 8 | 17 |

Many pupils will notice that the number of moves goes up in 2s.

Some may be able to find that

number of moves = number of counters in one line × 2 + 1 or
number of moves = total number of counters + 1 or
number of moves = total number of squares

Ask pupils if they can use algebraic shorthand to write down their rules, stating clearly what their letters stand for.

Some may be able to show that their rule is correct for any sized grid. One year 8 boy put it nicely: 'The number of moves is the number of counters plus 1 because one of counters wastes a move by going sideways – all the others go up or down.'

◊ One possible extension is to only allow one diagonal move, the rest being horizontal or vertical. The method for the least number of moves in this case is harder to find and to describe. The rule is $n = 4c - 1$ where $n$ is the number of moves and $c$ is the number of counters in one line. The initial moves for 4 counters in one line are

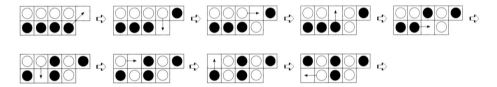

### B4  Cutting a cake (p 97)

◊ Emphasise that each cut must go from one side of the cake to another.
For example, these cuts are not valid.

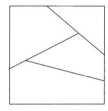

◊ Pupils could investigate the minimum and maximum number of pieces. The results are

| Number of cuts | Minimum number of pieces | Maximum number of pieces |
|---|---|---|
| 0 | 1 | 1 |
| 1 | 2 | 2 |
| 2 | 3 | 4 |
| 3 | 4 | 7 |
| 4 | 5 | 11 |
| 5 | 6 | 16 |
| 6 | 7 | 22 |
| 7 | 8 | 29 |
| 8 | 9 | 37 |

◊ Encourage less confident pupils to consider the minimum number of pieces first.

◊ Pupils may comment that:
- The minimum number of pieces goes up by 1 each time.
- The minimum number of pieces is always 1 more than the number of cuts (or, with $n$ cuts, the minimum number of pieces is $n + 1$).
- The minimum number of pieces can be achieved by making a set of parallel cuts.
- The maximum numbers of pieces goes up by 1, then 2, then 3 and so on.

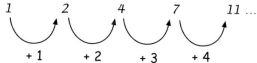

- To achieve the maximum number of pieces, take the previous diagram and make a cut that crosses each of the previous cuts.
- The sequence of numbers for the maximum number of pieces for one or more cuts (2, 4, 7, 11, 16, 22, …) can be found by adding 1 to each of the numbers in the sequence for the maximum number of crossing points in *Crossing points* (1, 3, 6, 10, 15, 21, …).

◊ Pupils may correctly predict the maximum number of pieces for various numbers of cuts but find it difficult to produce the corresponding diagrams. Using larger squares may help.

◊ For any number of cuts all numbers of pieces between the minimum and maximum can be achieved. Each diagram can be found by altering the previous one. For example, with four cuts:

5 pieces   6 pieces   7 pieces   8 pieces   9 pieces   10 pieces   11 pieces

## B5 Spots in a square (p 98)

◊ Emphasise that, if lines cross over, this has to be treated as creating more spots, for example

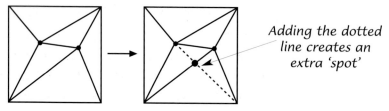

Adding the dotted line creates an extra 'spot'

◊ The results up to 6 spots (including 0 spots) are

| Number of spots | Number of triangles |
|:---:|:---:|
| 0 | 2 |
| 1 | 4 |
| 2 | 6 |
| 3 | 8 |
| 4 | 10 |
| 5 | 12 |
| 6 | 14 |

Many pupils will notice that the number of triangles goes up in 2s.
Some may see that

number of triangles = number of spots × 2 + 2 or

number of triangles = (number of spots + 1) × 2

◊ Some pupils may realise that, given any diagram, you can add a spot in the middle of one of the triangles and join it to the three vertices of the triangles. This creates 3 smaller triangles inside the larger one, hence increasing the overall number of triangles by 2.
For example,

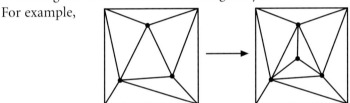

If a spot is added to an existing line, the two new lines will each add one to the number of the triangles.

## B6 Turn, turn, turn (p 98)

This is a very rich activity with many possibilities for extension.
Encourage pupils to follow their own lines of enquiry but some may need help in formulating questions.

Optional: Square dotty paper

◊ Many have found it beneficial for pupils to walk through the instructions to draw a turning track, emphasising the 90° turn each time.

◊ Encourage pupils to investigate questions such as:
  • Do you always get back to your starting point?
    If you do, how many times do you repeat the instructions?
  • What difference does it make if you turn left instead of right each time?
  • What shape are the tracks?
    Do you get different types of tracks with different sets of numbers?

- Why do some tracks have 'holes' while others have 'overlaps'?

hole

overlap

Can you predict whether or not a track will have a hole or an overlap from the set of three numbers? Can you predict the size of the hole?

- What will happen with sets of consecutive numbers?
- What if you look at sets of numbers where the first two are always the same?
- What happens if you change the order of the numbers? Will the track for 1, 2, 4 look like the track for 4, 1, 2 for example?
- What if two or more of the numbers are the same?

◊ Pupils may notice these facts.

- It doesn't matter what order the numbers are in. You always produce the same track although it may be rotated or reflected.
- Turning left produces a reflection of the turning right track.
- If the numbers are all the same, you get a square track.
- If two of the numbers are the same, you get a cross shape.
- All tracks made with three numbers have rotation symmetry.
- If the two smallest numbers add up to the largest, you get a track with no hole or overlap.
  For example,

1, 3, 2 (right turn)

1, 3, 2 (left turn)

7, 3, 4 (right turn)

- If the sum of the two smallest numbers is greater than the largest number, you get a 'windmill' shape with an overlap.
  For example,

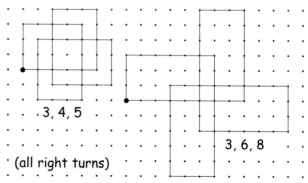

3, 4, 5

(all right turns)

3, 6, 8

- If the sum of the two smallest numbers is smaller than the largest number, you get a windmill shape with a hole.
  For example,

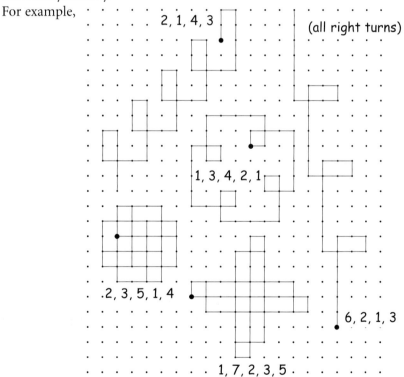

·1, 5, 2

(all right turns)

·3, 2, 6

The size of the hole is the largest number minus the sum of the two smallest numbers.

◊ Investigating longer sets of numbers, pupils will find that 4 numbers produce infinite 'spiral' tracks and 5 numbers produce 'closed' tracks with rotation symmetry.
  For example,

2, 1, 4, 3

(all right turns)

1, 3, 4, 2, 1

2, 3, 5, 1, 4

6, 2, 1, 3

1, 7, 2, 3, 5

◊ Pupils can investigate what happens if you change the turning angle. For example, you could use a 60° right turn and investigate on trianglular spotty paper.

◊ Pupils can use LOGO to draw their turning tracks.

# Think of a number

This unit develops the important idea of an inverse process and shows how to use this idea to solve an equation. 'Think of a number' puzzles are the context.

In later work, pupils should realise the limitations of using arrow diagrams to solve equations. The 'balancing' method should then become the principal method for solving equations.

In this unit, arrow diagrams are drawn with circles and ellipses. Pupils may find it easier to use squares and rectangles in their diagrams.

| | | |
|---|---|---|
| **T** | p 99 **A** Number puzzles | Using arrow diagrams and inverses to solve 'think of a number' puzzles |
| **T** | p 102 **B** Using letters | Writing number puzzles as equations |
| **T** | p 104 **C** Solving equations | Solving linear equations using arrows diagrams and inverses |
| **T** | p 105 **D** Quick solve | A game to consolidate solving equations |

| **Essential** | **Optional** |
|---|---|
| Calculators | Sheet 160 |
| Sheet 159 | |
| **Practice booklet** pages 38 to 40 | |

## A Number puzzles (p 99)

> Calculators for working with decimals and large numbers

**T**

◊ You could introduce this section by asking the pupils to each think of a number without telling anyone what it is.

Now ask them to

Add 1.
Multiply by 3.
Add 5.
Take away 2.
Divide by 2.

*'This introduction went down very well. By giving simple numbers and carefully timing when I asked them I was able to get even the weakest to respond.'*

Ask some pupils to tell you what their answers are and then work backwards to give the numbers they were thinking of.

Pupils could discuss how they think you worked them out.

Now, give some single-operation problems such as

> I think of a number.
> I multiply by 9 and my answer is 216.
> What number did I think of?

Ensure discussion of these brings out the idea of using an inverse and arrow diagrams.

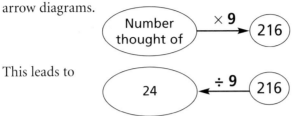

This leads to

Encourage pupils to check each solution by substituting in the original puzzle.

Now move on to 'think of a number' problems that use more than one operation and show how arrow diagrams and inverses can be used to solve them.

Many pupils will feel more confident using 'trial and improvement' to solve these problems. To demonstrate the power of using inverses, include problems involving decimals and many operations. For example

> I think of a number.
> I divide by 5.
> I subtract 45.
> I multiply by 1.2 .
> I add 8.
> I multiply by 0.2 .
> I subtract 12.
> My answer is 10.
> What number did I think of?

Pupils could use both trial-and-improvement and inverse methods and compare them.

You could end this teacher-led session by asking the pupils to solve the puzzles on the pupil page. The solutions to these puzzles are 17, 12 and 3.3 respectively.

## B **Using letters** (p 102)

'Very good …
needed to refresh use
of brackets first.'

It may help to tell pupils that this section is not about solving the puzzles or equations, but about linking equations, arrow diagrams and puzzles. Otherwise, they may feel that they have not fully answered the questions unless they have 'solved' each puzzle to find the number thought of.

The questions could be used as a basis for a whole-class discussion.

◊ Include some examples where multiplication is the first operation and some where it is the second operation. Pupils may take some time to understand when they need to use brackets. You could include the puzzle and diagrams leading to the equation $2n + 3 = 20$ bringing out how it differs from $2(n + 3) = 20$ (the example on page 102).

◊ Make sure pupils know that $2 \times (n + 3)$ is the same as $(n + 3) \times 2$ and that $2(n + 3)$ is shorthand for it.

**B1** Watch out for pupils who match up A with X to start with.

## C **Solving equations** (p 104)

> Calculators for working with decimals and large numbers

◊ In your discussion, include the equation $2n - 3 = 130$ and compare it with $2(n - 3) = 130$ on page 104.

◊ The equations in question C5 involve more than two operations. It may be beneficial to include some examples of this kind in your introduction.

## D **Quick solve** (p 105)

The version of this game described in the pupil's book can be played in groups of three or four. It can also be played as a whole class or individually (see below).

> Each group needs a set of 36 cards (sheet 159).
> Optional: Each pupil needs a copy of sheet 160 if they check each other's answers. Note that sheets 159 and 160 look similar to sheets 157 and 158. Care should be taken not to confuse them.

◊ Emphasise that **all** players take a card at the start of the game and take another as soon as they think they have solved their equation. They should keep their equation cards – they will not be used by another player.

◊ There are other ways to use the cards.

### One pile version

This is played as the version in the book but pupils take cards from a mixed shuffled pile.

### Three pile whole-class version

The game could be played as a whole class with the teacher having sets of cards in three piles: cards worth 1 point, 2 points and 3 points.

Individual pupils ask the teacher for a 1, 2 or 3 point card. When they think they have solved the equation, they ask for another card.

Continue until all the cards have been taken or some specified time limit has been reached.

## One pile whole-class version

This is played as the three pile whole-class version but pupils take cards at random from a mixed pile.

## Individual version

The cards do not need to be cut out for this version. Each pupil solves as many equations as they can from the set of 36 in a specified time. Solutions are checked and points awarded as before.

The game can be played with the number of points awarded for a correct solution being the value of the solution.

A set of solutions is given below.

| | | | |
|---|---|---|---|
| Card 1 | $n = 2$ | Card 19 | $n = 13.5$ |
| Card 2 | $n = 5$ | Card 20 | $n = 30$ |
| Card 3 | $n = 4$ | Card 21 | $n = 18$ |
| Card 4 | $n = 18$ | Card 22 | $n = 25$ |
| Card 5 | $n = 3$ | Card 23 | $n = 0$ |
| Card 6 | $n = 4$ | Card 24 | $n = 27$ |
| Card 7 | $n = 5$ | Card 25 | $n = 7.6$ |
| Card 8 | $n = 4$ | Card 26 | $n = 3.8$ |
| Card 9 | $n = 3$ | Card 27 | $n = 12$ |
| Card 10 | $n = 1$ | Card 28 | $n = 3.2$ |
| Card 11 | $n = 6$ | Card 29 | $n = 2$ |
| Card 12 | $n = 3$ | Card 30 | $n = 6.5$ |
| Card 13 | $n = 1.5$ | Card 31 | $n = 10$ |
| Card 14 | $n = 2.5$ | Card 32 | $n = 3$ |
| Card 15 | $n = 10$ | Card 33 | $n = 3$ |
| Card 16 | $n = 13$ | Card 34 | $n = 6.4$ |
| Card 17 | $n = 9$ | Card 35 | $n = 2.3$ |
| Card 18 | $n = 0.5$ | Card 36 | $n = 2.5$ |

**A1**

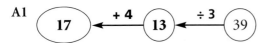

The number thought of was 17.

**A2** (a) Puzzle 1: C   Puzzle 2: B

(b) Puzzle 1

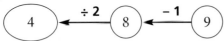

The number thought of was 4.

Puzzle 2

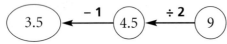

The number thought of was 3.5.

**A3** (a) I think of a number.
  • I divide by 5.
  • I take away 7.
  The result is 17.
  What number did I think of?

(b)

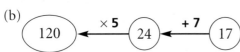

The number thought of was 120.

**A4** (a)

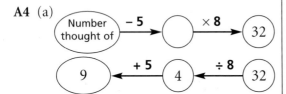

The number thought of was 9.

(b)

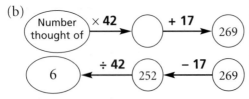

The number thought of was 6.

(c)

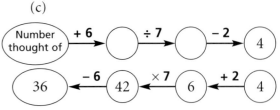

The number thought of was 36.

(d)

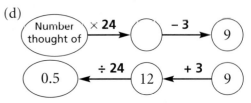

The number thought of was 0.5.

(e)

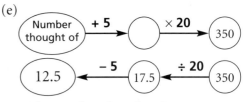

The number thought of was 12.5.

**A5** Using positive whole numbers and zero gives the following possibilities.
  • I add 10, I multiply by 1.
  • I add 4, I multiply by 2.
  • I add 2, I multiply by 3.
  • I add 1, I multiply by 4.
  • I add 0, I multiply by 6.

Extending to negative numbers and decimals gives an infinite number of possibilities.

**A6** The pupil's puzzles

Ⓑ **Using letters** (p 102)

**B1** (a) A: Z,  B: V,  C: Y,  D: X

(b)

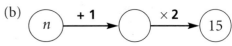

**B2** (a) Puzzle 1: E   Puzzle 2: C
  Puzzle 3: B   Puzzle 4: D

(b) I think of a number.
  • I subtract 2.
  • I multiply by 5.
  The result is 8.
  What number did I think of?

**B3** (a) $3n + 4 = 108$

(b) $16n = 52$

(c) $6(n - 5) = 42$

**B4** (a) $5(n + 3) = 20$

(b) $9k - 3 = 15$

**B5** (a)

(b)

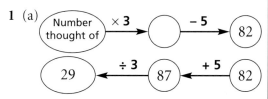

ℂ **Solving equations** (p 104)

**C1** (a) $n = 14$   (b) $h = 25$   (c) $m = 21$

(d) $x = 13$   (e) $p = 16$   (f) $z = 5$

**C2** (a) $m = 2.5$   (b) $a = 3.5$   (c) $n = 4.2$

(d) $p = 5.6$   (e) $x = 7.5$   (f) $y = 12.6$

**C3** $(2 \times 6) + 4 = 12 + 4 = 16$
The pupil's equations with solution $n = 6$

**C4** The pupil's equations with solution
$y = 1.5$

***C5** (a) $m = 23$   (b) $q = 5$   (c) $p = 0.05$

**What progress have you made?** (p 106)

**1** (a)

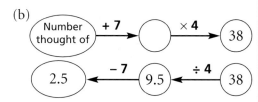

The number thought of was 29.

(b)

The number thought of was 2.5.

**2** A: Z   B: W   C: Y

**3** (a) $z = 37$   (b) $p = 32$   (c) $y = 5.5$

(d) $x = 1.2$   (e) $q = 85$

**Practice booklet**

**Section A** (p 38)

The pupil's arrow diagrams leading to the
following answers:

**1** 11        **2** 31

**3** 7         **4** 136

**5** 2.5       **6** 0.5

**7** 21        **8** 1.5

**Section B** (p 39)

**1** (a) $14n = 56$      (b) $5n - 7 = 103$

(c) $3(n + 4) = 54$  (d) $17(n - 8) = 68$

**2** (a) $7p - 4 = 31$   (b) $3(s + 8) = 33$

(c) $6(q - 5) = 60$  (d) $4m - 11 = 37$

***3** $4(11n + 2) = 96$

**Section C** (p 40)

**1** The pupil's arrow diagrams leading to
the following answers:

(a) $x = 9$    (b) $h = 12$   (c) $d = 7$

(d) $k = 19$   (e) $p = 19$   (f) $s = 7$

(g) $q = 4$    (h) $m = 11$   (i) $v = 21$

(j) $n = 15$

**2** (a) $y = 2.5$   (b) $w = 4.5$   (c) $h = 6.5$

(d) $b = 9.5$   (e) $c = 1.5$   (f) $z = 3.6$

(g) $p = 1.8$   (h) $q = 3.5$   (i) $t = 1.3$

(j) $x = 2.7$

**3** (a) $n = 5.1$   (b) $a = 3.3$   (c) $d = 2.4$

(d) $c = 8.2$   (e) $a = 1.5$   (f) $w = 6.5$

(g) $h = 6.1$   (h) $p = 0.2$   (i) $q = 6.9$

(j) $x = 2.5$

**4** The pupil's equations with solution
$m = 5$

**5** The pupil's equations with solution $x = 1$

**6** The pupil's equations with solution
$p = 2.5$

# ⑭ Practical problems

These use equipment so need to be done in class. Pupils need not do all the tasks: just doing some will tell you a lot about how well they can measure, estimate and apply number skills in problem solving.

One approach is to set up a 'circus' of tables; on each table is the equipment for one task and a label giving its name and page number (tasks with readily available equipment can be duplicated on more than one table). Pupils move round the circus following the instructions in the pupil's book. It is a good idea to have some 'exercise' work ready in case there is a log-jam as pupils go around the circus.

Alternatively, you can set up just one task (possibly in duplicate), and while the rest of the class get on with written work individuals or small groups come out in turn to do it.

'Weighty problems' is for a small group of pupils; the others can be done individually or in pairs.

Many pupils find weighing difficult, whether interpreting scale graduations on mechanical scales or coping with decimal places on digital balances. So it may be a good idea to add some straightforward weighing to the collection of tasks.

### Weighty problems (p 107)

> Scales or electronic balance
> Two stones, say about 4 cm and 8 cm in diameter
> A collection of familiar objects, including one with its weight clearly marked on it (for example a 500 g or 1 kg bag of sugar)

◊ In task 1 each group's estimates could be displayed on a dot plot (see 'Comparisons') and ideas of spread and over- or under-estimation discussed by the class. It is a good idea if everybody in the group checks the reading on the scales when the stones are weighed.

◊ After task 2 pupils could discuss ways of deciding which estimated order of weights was the best.

A related activity that goes well is for a pupil to hold the object of known weight (bag of sugar or whatever) in one hand and a different object in the other; the pupil estimates the weight of the other object then checks by weighing.

## Beans (p 107)

> Two identical large sweet jars with lids, one empty and the other at least half filled with dried beans or pasta shapes with its lid taped down (butter beans are suitable, but not red kidney beans or other varieties that are poisonous when uncooked)
> About 100 extra beans or pasta shapes of the type in the jar
> An electronic balance or scales sensitive enough to weigh a few grams

◊ These are two approaches pupils have used to start solving the problem.
- Putting a layer of the extra beans into the empty jar and measuring the layer's height.
- Finding the weight of the beans in the jar by subtracting the weight of the empty jar.

In the second case, some go on to weigh a single bean. If so, ask them to check whether the beans have the same or different weights. If they have different weights, can pupils suggest a way to deal with this?

## Cornflakes (p 108)

> A full box of cornflakes, with its price
> A cereal bowl
> An electronic balance or scales

◊ Some pupils may need a hint to work out the weight of the cornflakes without the bowl.

◊ You could extend the work to comparing the cost of different types of cereal or comparing the cost of a serving-sized box with that of the same amount of cereal in a full-sized box.

## Getting better (p 108)

> A 5 ml spoon labelled 5 ml
> A container with a scale graduated in ml
> Three different sized medicine bottles (one less than 60 ml) distinguished by colour or labelling, but without their capacities marked
> Water, a tray and some paper towels

◊ A prepared answer sheet may help weaker pupils.

◊ Follow-up might include
- discussion of the appropriate level of accuracy
- estimation of capacity from knowing that 1 cm cube has a volume of a millilitre and a 10 cm cube has a volume of a litre
- estimation by pupils, perhaps as a homework assignment, of their daily fluid intake

# Chocolate (p 109)

This is a problem-solving activity in which pupils can use their
knowledge and understanding of fractions, decimals and/or percentages.

| Essential | Optional |
|---|---|
| 6 bars or blocks of something which can be divided up and shared out equally | Bars of chocolate (of a kind not already subdivided into portions) |
| **Practice booklet** pages 41 to 44 | |

**T**

◊ The activities and problems are all variations of this basic idea:
  • A number of tables are set out with some chocolate bars.
  • A group of pupils are asked, one by one, to choose a table to sit at.
  • When everyone has sat at a table, the bars on each table are shared
    equally between those at that table.

The problem for the pupils is to decide which table to sit at in the hope of
getting the most chocolate at the shareout.

**Getting started**

◊ It is best to start with a fairly simple situation. For example,
distribute 6 chocolate bars on three tables as shown.

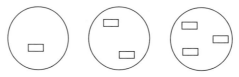

(or start with 2 tables and fewer bars)

Choose a group of pupils to take part, say eight, and explain the problem.
Ask them one by one to choose their table (they cannot change their minds
later).

◊ As pupils choose where to sit, involve the whole class and ask questions
such as:
  • Where would you sit? Why?
  • How much chocolate would each person get at this table if no one else
    sits here?
  • Is it best to be the first to choose, the last, or doesn't it matter?

◊ Once the last pupil has chosen, ask pupils to decide who gets the most
chocolate and to justify their answer. Explanations could involve
  • comparing fractions, decimals or percentages

*'I thought this would
be chaos and pupils
would gain little from
it. In fact, lots of useful
discussion was
generated! Had I
remembered to buy
the chocolate it would
have been even better.
(We used sheets of
paper to represent
chocolate.)'*

*'I split the class into
three teams. Each
team in turn sent one
person to sit at the
tables. The aim was
for one team to get the
most chocolate.'*

- comparing ratios
- imagining the bars made of an appropriate number of squares and comparing the number of squares each pupil gets
- imagining the bars are a particular weight and comparing the weight of chocolate each pupil gets

Pupils can choose their own approach or you can ask them to concentrate on one aspect, say fractions or decimals.

### Variations

◊ Obviously the number of tables and bars can be varied.

You could also tell pupils that you will decide beforehand how many pupils will sit down but they will not know this until you stop them and they then share out the chocolate.

### Follow-up work

◊ Pupils could work in small groups on particular problems. Examples are
- For the last person to sit down from a group of eight, what are all the possibilities? Are some of these possibilities more likely than others?
- Which is the best table for the first person to sit at?
- Which final seating arrangements give everyone more than half a bar of chocolate?
- Which seating arrangements are the 'fairest'?

◊ The practice booklet provides some follow-up questions but you may need to select. For example, questions involving fractions will not be appropriate for pupils who have used decimals throughout.

### Practice booklet (p 41)

Explanations are given here using fractions but other explanations are possible (for example, using percentages).

1 $\frac{1}{2}$

2 25%

3 40 g

4 (a) Table P: $\frac{1}{2}$   Table Q: $\frac{2}{3}$
  (b) Table Q

5 (a) Q       (b) Q       (c) P

6 (a) Join table A to get the most chocolate. Joining table A would give you $\frac{3}{4}$ of a bar but joining table B would only give you $\frac{1}{2}$ of a bar.

  (b) Join table A to get the most chocolate. Joining table A would give you $\frac{2}{3}$ of a bar but joining table B would only give you $\frac{3}{5}$ of a bar.

7 (a) Join table P to get the most chocolate. Joining table P would give you $\frac{3}{4}$ of a bar but joining table Q would only give you $\frac{2}{3}$ of a bar.

(b) Join table Q to get the most chocolate. Joining table Q would give you $\frac{1}{2}$ of a bar but joining table P would only give you $\frac{1}{3}$ of a bar.

(c) Join table Q to get the most chocolate. Joining table Q would give you $\frac{1}{3}$ of a bar but joining table P would only give you $\frac{3}{10}$ of a bar.

(d) Join table P to get the most chocolate. Joining table P would give you $\frac{9}{10}$ of a bar but joining table Q would only give you $\frac{4}{5}$ of a bar.

**8** (a) R    (b) P

**9** (a) Join table R to get the most chocolate. Joining table R would give you $\frac{3}{7}$ of a bar but joining table P or Q would only give you $\frac{1}{3}$ of a bar.

(b) Join table R to get the most chocolate. Joining table R would give you a whole bar but joining tables P, Q or S would only give you $\frac{1}{4}$, $\frac{2}{5}$ or $\frac{1}{2}$ of a bar.

**10** 6 people

**11** (a) 9 people  (b) 8 people  (c) 3 people

**12** (a) 2 bars  (b) 12 bars  (c) 3 bars

**13** 3 at table P and 6 at table Q

**14** 12 at table P and 8 at table Q

**15** 2 at table P and 3 at table Q giving 5 people in total. They will get 2 bars each.

**16** On the left, each person gets $\frac{3}{4}$ of a bar. On the right, if 5 people sat down they would each get more than $\frac{3}{4}$ of a bar; if 6 people sat they would get less than $\frac{3}{4}$ of a bar, so it can't be done.

# Review 2 (p 109)

1 (a) $3\frac{1}{2}$ hours      (b) 1:00 p.m.

  (c) 4:30 p.m.

2 (a)

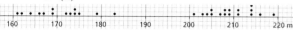

  (b) 64 mm   (c) 202 mm

  (d) The handspans are in two clusters.

3 (a) $9 \xrightarrow{\times 2} 18 \xrightarrow{+5} 23$

  (b) $2 \xrightarrow{\times \mathbf{9}} \mathbf{18} \xrightarrow{+14} 32$

4 (a) $s \xrightarrow{+2} s+2 \xrightarrow{\times 4} 4(s+2)$

  (b) $z \xrightarrow{\times 5} 5z \xrightarrow{+6} 5z+6$

  (c) $w \xrightarrow{-9} w-9 \xrightarrow{\times 3} 3(w-9)$

  (d) $p \xrightarrow{\times 4} 4p \xrightarrow{-7} 4p-7$

  (e) $h \xrightarrow{+9} h+9 \xrightarrow{\times 3} 3(h+9)$

5 (a) 3 m 20 cm      (b) 5 m 16 cm

  (c) 1 m 80 cm      (d) 4 m 9 cm

6 (a) 1.07 m   (b) 2.05 m

  (c) 2.8 m    (d) 7.08 m

7 (a) 625 cm   (b) 1251 cm

  (c) 630 cm   (d) 1003 cm

8 $\frac{1}{2}$ and 0.5, 0.4 and $\frac{2}{5}$, 0.8 and $\frac{4}{5}$, 0.2 and $\frac{1}{5}$

9 (a) 48   (b) 50.5   (c) 4   (d) 3

10 1.27 m

11 (a) 17 days   (b) 13 days   (c) 11 days

  (d) It does take 13 days. In fact a few more than $\frac{3}{4}$ have germinated by the 13th day.

12 (a) $4p+8$    (b) $3x-21$

  (c) $5d+25$   (d) $14+7t$

13 (a) $2a+8 = 2(a+\mathbf{4})$

  (b) $\mathbf{9}b-45 = 9(\mathbf{b}-5)$

  (c) $\mathbf{7}(s-2) = 7s-\mathbf{14}$

14 (a) 9.97    (b) 10.03

15 (a) 9.6     (b) 3.75

16 (a) 1.69 m   (b) 1.44 m   (c) 1.05 m

  (d) 1.28 m   (e) 1.06 m   (f) 1.06 m

17 They will take (c), (e) and (f).

18 36 cm

19 (a) $2n+9 = 23$, $n = 7$

  (b) $4(n-17) = 16$, $n = 21$

  (c) $6n-15 = 0$, $n = 2.5$

20 (a) $z = 12$   (b) $p = 1$

  (c) $d = 5.8$   (d) $x = 8.5$

## Mixed questions 2 (Practice booklet p 45)

1 (a) (i) 36 seconds   (ii) 37 seconds

  (b) (i) 50 seconds   (ii) 36 seconds

  (c) (i) True   (ii) False   (iii) False

2 (a) $3(p+5) = \mathbf{3}p+\mathbf{15}$   (b) $4q-12 = \mathbf{4}(q-\mathbf{3})$

  (c) $5(r-\mathbf{3}) = \mathbf{5}r-15$   (d) $\mathbf{7}s+42 = \mathbf{7}(s+6)$

3 (a) BENCH     (b) DESK

  (c) STOOL     (d) TABLE

4 David, Colin, Eric, Vicky, Sara

5 (a) 1.74 m   (b) 1.89 m   (c) 1.96 m

  (d) 2.03 m   (e) 2.17 m   (f) 2.25 m

6 1.05 m (or 1 m 5 cm)

7 (a) Yes     (b) 0.34 m (or 34 cm)

8 (a) 12   (b) 10   (c) 66   (d) 59.5

9 $2n+5 = 19$, $n = 7$

10 (a) $q = 7$   (b) $r = 8$   (c) $x = 24$

# ⑯ Multiplication and division

The unit is to be done without a calculator.

> **Practice booklet** pages 47 to 49

## Ⓐ Multiples of ten (p 112)

This is a quick revision of multiplying multiples of ten.

## Ⓑ Table method (p 112)

**T**

Many pupils prefer the table method because they can see clearly where each number comes from. The standard 'long multiplication' method is often carried out wrongly when memory fails.

◊ For the table for $12 \times 14$ you can ask where the 10 and the 4 come from, where the 100 comes from, and so on.

For $23 \times 34$ some pupils may find this helpful:

| × | 10 | 10 | 10 | 4 |
|---|-----|-----|-----|-----|
| 10 | 100 | 100 | 100 | 40 |
| 10 | 100 | 100 | 100 | 40 |
| 3 | 30 | 30 | 30 | 12 |

## Ⓒ Some ways of setting out multiplication (p 114)

**T**

Pupils can try to relate the table method to the 'long multiplication' method.

## Ⓓ Lattice method (p 114)

**T**

This is of historical interest and some pupils may well prefer it to other methods.

◊ Another method which may be of interest is the so-called 'Egyptian' method, which is based on doubling. You can write the table below on the board and ask pupils if they can use the numbers to work out $47 \times 59$.

| | |
|---|---|
| 1 | 59 |
| 2 | 118 |
| 4 | 236 |
| 8 | 472 |
| 16 | 944 |
| 32 | 1888 |

By breaking 47 down into $32 + 8 + 4 + 2 + 1$, they can work out $47 \times 59$ by adding 1888, 472, 236, 118 and 59.

## E Division with no remainders (p 115)

◊ In the introductory discussion make sure that pupils appreciate that 368 ÷ 23 can be thought of as '368 shared between 23' (sharing) as well as 'how many 23s in 368' (grouping).

◊ Pupils may have learned the standard 'long division' algorithm and be happy with it. But many do not find it straightforward and the 'chunking' method (Sheena's method) is a fairly efficient alternative.

◊ It may be worth practising mentally working out $17 \times 10$, $17 \times 20$, $17 \times 5$ as this is useful when using the 'chunking' method.

◊ The example 325 ÷ 13 can be used to illustrate dealing first with a chunk of twenty 13s, followed by a chunk of five 13s.

## F Division with remainders (p 116)

◊ In the initial discussion pupils should understand that in the example, when the final chunk of 52 is taken from 91, 39 is left over and is the remainder.

### A Multiples of ten (p 112)

**A1** (a) 800  (b) 900  (c) 1200
(d) 150  (e) 1400  (f) 2000
(g) 1000  (h) 630  (i) 4800
(j) 4000

**A2** (a) 6000  (b) 12 000  (c) 8000
(d) 42 000  (e) 2700  (f) 2000
(g) 48 000  (h) 20 000  (i) 60 000
(j) 30 000

**A3** (a) 60  (b) 50  (c) 900
(d) 8  (e) 400  (f) 5

### B Table method (p 112)

**B1** $13 \times 12$

| ×  | 10  | 2  |
|----|-----|----|
| 10 | 100 | 20 |
| 3  | 30  | 6  |

```
  100
+  20
+  30
+   6
  156
```

**B2** $14 \times 15$

| ×  | 10  | 5  |
|----|-----|----|
| 10 | 100 | 50 |
| 4  | 40  | 20 |

```
  100
+  50
+  40
+  20
  210
```

**B3** $16 \times 23$

| ×  | 20  | 3  |
|----|-----|----|
| 10 | 200 | 30 |
| 6  | 120 | 18 |

```
  200
+  30
+ 120
+  18
  368
```

**B4** $24 \times 35$

| ×  | 30  | 5   |
|----|-----|-----|
| 20 | 600 | 100 |
| 4  | 120 | 20  |

```
  600
+ 100
+ 120
+  20
  840
```

**B5** $43 \times 64$

| ×  | 60   | 4   |
|----|------|-----|
| 40 | 2400 | 160 |
| 3  | 180  | 12  |

```
 2400
+ 160
+ 180
+  12
 2752
```

**B6** $53 \times 148$

| ×  | 100  | 40   | 8   |
|----|------|------|-----|
| 50 | 5000 | 2000 | 400 |
| 3  | 300  | 120  | 24  |

```
 5000
+ 2000
+  400
+  300
+  120
+   24
 7844
```

**B7** $362 \times 47$

| × | 40 | 7 |
|---|---|---|
| 300 | 12000 | 2100 |
| 60 | 2400 | 420 |
| 2 | 80 | 14 |

+ 2100
+ 2400
+ 420
+ 80
+ 14
17014

**B8** The pupil's two multiplications

### C Some ways of setting out multiplication (p 114)

**C1** (a) 585 (b) 1512 (c) 1692
(d) 2756

**C2** (a) 2475 (b) 2916 (c) 3564
(d) 3936

### D Lattice method (p 114)

**D1** (a) $13 \times 14$

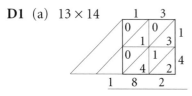

$13 \times 14 = 182$

(b) $24 \times 38$

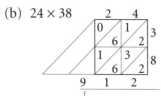

$24 \times 38 = 912$

(c) $215 \times 34$

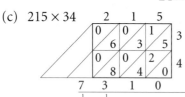

$215 \times 34 = 7310$

(d) $35 \times 107$

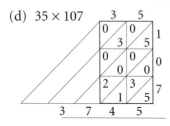

$35 \times 107 = 3745$

(e) $246 \times 458$

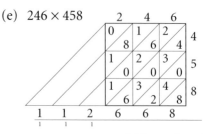

$246 \times 458 = 112\,668$

**D2** The largest is $72 \times 53 = 3816$.
The smallest is $37 \times 25 = 925$.

### E Division with no remainders (p 115)

**E1** (a) 6 (b) 8 (c) 7 (d) 8
(e) 12 (f) 16 (g) 18 (h) 21

**E2** 25

**E3** 21

**E4** 28

**E5** £7

**E6** £56

**E7** 76

**E8** The pupil's problem in words

**E9** The pupil's problems in words

**E10** (a) 21 (b) 17 (c) 38

### F Division with remainders (p 116)

**F1** (a) 12 r 3 (b) 11 r 19 (c) 19 r 5
(d) 16 r 23 (e) 19 r 16 (f) 9 r 12
(g) 15 r 24 (h) 26 r 46

**F2** CABBAGE

**F3** The pupil's word puzzle

**F4** Two of them do (21 and 23).

**F5** He needs 17 packets.
He will have 6 more rolls than he needs.

**F6** He can make 21 necklaces.
He will have 34 beads left over.

**F7** 1279

**F8**  48

**F9**  1

**F10**  155 seconds

**F11**  39 minutes and 10 seconds

**F12**  4 hours and 40 minutes

### What progress have you made? (p 117)

1  (a)  1200      (b)  30 000
   (c)  24 000     (d)  120 000

2  (a)  1938      (b)  1288
   (c)  10 810     (d)  7448

3  (a)  22     (b)  13     (c)  19

4  (a)  17 r 11   (b)  23 r 10   (c)  41 r 1

5  28

## Practice booklet

### Sections A and B (p 47)

1  (a)  1400      (b)  12 000     (c)  240 000
   (d)  4000

2  (a)  192       (b)  182        (c)  165

3  (a)  408       (b)  1035       (c)  2170

4  (a)  5781      (b)  12 792      (c)  21 105

5  (a)  255       (b)  756        (c)  1665
   (d)  2784      (e)  7344       (f)  3564
   (g)  10 224     (h)  29 322

### Sections C and D (p 48)

1  (a)  378       (b)  1568       (c)  2209
   (d)  1350      (e)  1825       (f)  2738
   (g)  2835      (h)  3484       (i)  4556
   (j)  6006      (k)  6468       (l)  15 778

2  The largest is $81 \times 64 = 5184$.
   The smallest is $16 \times 48 = 768$.

3  (a)  224       (b)  221        (c)  1504
   (d)  936       (e)  6164       (f)  10 664
   (g)  97 812     (h)  104 755

4  (a)  $16 \times 52 = 832$ pints
   (b)  $16 \times 12 = £192$
   (c)  $24 \times 48 = 1152$ miles
   (d)  $312 \times 45 = 14 040$ copies

## Section E (p 49)

1  (a)  4     (b)  11   (c)  15   (d)  13

2  12

3  26

4  8

5  The pupil's problems

## Section F (p 49)

1  (a)  6 r 11      (b)  12 r 2
   (c)  21 r 10     (d)  19 r 21

2  BEACH

3  The pupil's word puzzle

4  14 packets are needed.
   There will be 16 spare pencils

5  They can make 14 chains.
   There will be 15 links left over

# 17 Approximation

> **Practice booklet** pages 50 and 51

## Ⓐ Numbers in the news (p 118)

◊ Each news extract has an exact number in the text but a rough approximation in the headline. Ask why this is done.
You could give some exact numbers and ask for suggestions for rough approximations. The short exercise includes this and also working the other way from a headline to a possible exact figure.

To finish off, or for homework, you could ask pupils to make up both a story and the headline.

**A3** Depending on the ability of the group, you could look at a number of different answers to each part of the question and discuss what the largest or smallest figure in the story might be for the headline still to apply.

For example, in part (a) if the cyclist's actual trip were 3690 miles, the headline would be more likely to say '3700'. Where would the dividing line be between headlines of 3600 and 3700?

## Ⓑ Rounding to the nearest hundred (p 121)

◊ You may need to revise rounding to the nearest ten.
The number line is very useful when explaining rounding.

## Ⓒ Rounding to the nearest thousand (p 122)

## Ⓓ Rounding decimals (p 123)

◊ You may need to emphasise that rounding, say, 4.697 to two decimal places gives 4.70, not just 4.7. The rounded results must have the number of places stated.

## Ⓐ Numbers in the news (p 118)

**A1** It is easier for the reader to 'take in' the rounded number.

**A2** The pupil's headlines including

(a) 37 000 or 40 000

(b) 25 000      (c) 2000

(d) 370 000 or nearly 400 000

**A3** The pupil's sentences

## Ⓑ Rounding to the nearest hundred (p 121)

**B1** 2600

**B2** (a) 1900    (b) 1900    (c) 1800

(d) 2400    (e) 2100

**B3** (a) 500    (b) 2000    (c) 2100

(d) 13 100    (e) 54 300

**B4** (a) 700    (b) 1400    (c) 1900

(d) 2500    (e) 25 000

**B5** (a)
| | |
|---|---|
| Pierre St-Martin | 4400 |
| Jean Bernard | 4300 |
| Cellagua | 3200 |
| Corchia | 3100 |
| Kacherlschact | 3000 |
| Holloch | 2700 |
| Snieznej | 2600 |

(b)

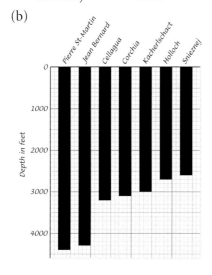

## Ⓒ Rounding to the nearest thousand (p 122)

**C1** (a) 6000    (b) 12 000    (c) 19 000

(d) 20 000    (e) 47 000    (f) 5000

(g) 75 000    (h) 286 000    (i) 842 000

(j) 740 000

**C2** (a) Manchester Utd, Liverpool, Arsenal, Newcastle Utd, Aston Villa, Chelsea

(b) Newcastle Utd and Aston Villa appear equal (both 36 000).

**C3**

| Division | Attendance |
|---|---|
| Premier | 10 805 000 |
| 1 | 6 932 000 |
| 2 | 3 195 000 |
| 3 | 1 852 000 |

**C4** (a) 31 000    (b) 7000    (c) 135 000

(d) 135 000    (e) 416 000    (f) 45 000

(g) 100 000    (h) 10 000

## Ⓓ Rounding decimals (p 123)

**D1** (a) 2.4    (b) 2.1

**D2** (a) 4.3    (b) 7.3    (c) 5.4

(d) 2.2    (e) 12.5

**D3** (a) 1.7    (b) 1.0    (c) 4.4

(d) 7.9    (e) 10.9

**D4** (a) 3.74    (b) 3.79    (c) 3.81

**D5** (a) 3.57    (b) 21.43    (c) 14.04

(d) 16.60    (e) 20.57

**D6** (a) 1.63    (b) 17.41    (c) 9.02

(d) 11.50    (e) 19.10

**D7** Piece A   9.64 cm
Piece B   4.11 cm
Piece C   5.40 cm

**D8** (a) 4.64    (b) 17.30    (c) 0.16

(d) 3.29    (e) 0.54

**D9** (a) 1.477    (b) 3.243    (c) 2.504
    (d) 2.760    (e) 3.158    (f) 2.861
    (g) 6.200    (h) 41.367    (i) 0.009
    (j) 0.004

**D10** (a) 8.7    (b) 45.70    (c) 2.31
    (d) 3.414    (e) 67.054    (f) 0.01

**D11** (a) 151.67    (b) 1.8    (c) 0.611
    (d) 1.7    (e) 0.316    (f) 130.7

## What progress have you made? (p 130)

1 7530

2 13 800

3 24 100

4 14 000

5 417 900

6 418 000

7 4.8

8 59.90

9 8.054

## Practice booklet

## Section B (p 50)

1 (a) 800    (b) 100    (c) 2500
   (d) 1100    (e) 200    (f) 5100
   (g) 3300    (h) 2100    (i) 3000
   (j) 1400

2 (a) 400    (b) 82 500    (c) 18 400
   (d) 11 100    (e) 4000    (f) 13 100
   (g) 29 700    (h) 76 200    (i) 7400
   (j) 44 400

3

|  | Calais | Santander |
| --- | --- | --- |
| Barcelona | 900 | 400 |
| Alicante | 1200 | 500 |
| Marbella | 1400 | 600 |
| Lisbon | 1300 | 600 |
| Faro | 1400 | 700 |

## Section C (p 50)

1 (a) 9000    (b) 1000    (c) 33 000
   (d) 25 000    (e) 13 000    (f) 873 000
   (g) 436 000    (h) 300 000    (i) 85 000
   (j) 405 000

2

| Cruise ship | Size in gross tons |
| --- | --- |
| Arcadia | 64 000 |
| Dawn Princess | 77 000 |
| Royal Princess | 45 000 |
| Minerva | 13 000 |
| Oriana | 70 000 |
| Island Princess | 20 000 |
| Grand Princess | 109 000 |

## Section D (p 51)

1 (a) 98.5    (b) 0.9    (c) 7.8
   (d) 10.1    (e) 4.3    (f) 11.3
   (g) 15.4    (h) 0.4    (i) 21.5
   (j) 20.1

2 (a) 76.6    (b) 60.8    (c) 12.8
   (d) 15.0    (e) 1.8    (f) 4.5
   (g) 4.7    (h) 0.5

3 (a) 7.27    (b) 3.61    (c) 42.74
   (d) 49.20    (e) 12.49    (f) 0.20
   (g) 36.10    (h) 48.20    (i) 4.35
   (j) 19.05

4 (a) 2.58    (b) 27.93    (c) 1.02
   (d) 24.29    (e) 5.49    (f) 4.41
   (g) 0.42    (h) 0.43

5 3.4176 and 3.4225

6 (a) 2.649    (b) 7.433    (c) 0.373
   (d) 3.710    (e) 5.931    (f) 0.600
   (g) 0.203    (h) 1.050    (i) 7.834
   (j) 1.301

7 (a) 7.726    (b) 36.557    (c) 11.949
   (d) 17.741    (e) 1.707    (f) 3.079
   (g) 4.679    (h) 0.870

8 6.3095 and 6.3102

# ⑱ Decimal calculation

This unit covers addition and subtraction of decimals up to two decimal places without a calculator.

Multiplication and division is by single-digit numbers and powers of ten without a calculator and by decimals with a calculator. The ideas of unit cost and 'best buy' are included.

| | | |
|---|---|---|
| **T** | p 125 **A** One decimal place | Calculating with decimals to one decimal place, without a calculator |
| **T** | p 127 **B** Two decimal places | Calculating with decimals to two decimal places, without a calculator |
| | p 130 **C** Multiplying and dividing by 10, 100, 1000, … | |
| **T** | p 131 **D** Metric units | Kilograms, grams, kilometres, metres, centimetres, litres, millilitres |
| **T** | p 132 **E** Buying food | Multiplying by a decimal with a calculator |
| **T** | p 133 **F** Unit cost | Dividing by a decimal to find unit costs and 'best buy' |
| | p 134 **G** Mixed questions | |

---

**Optional**
Sheet 125

**Practice booklet** pages 52 to 61

---

##  **One decimal place** (p 125)

◊ The teacher-led introduction should include discussion of both mental and written methods. The numbers in the loop can be used for this and some examples of suitable questions (which you can supplement with your own) are shown beside the loop. You could ask pupils to make up some questions of their own for other pupils to answer, from these numbers or from further loops.

Include mental work such as

- $12.4 + 0.1$
- $0.8 + 0.2$ (decimal complements in 1)
- $1.3 - 0.9$
- $1.6 \times 2$ (doubles of two-digit decimals)
- $0.2 \times 8$
- $7 \div 2$

Include work on standard column procedures for adding and subtracting.

◊ A suggestion for a game for two players called 'One or two' (not shown in the pupil's book) is given below.

**One or two**

| Sheet 125 (one set of cards per pair) |
| --- |

◊ Each pair puts a set of cards from sheet 125 face up on the table.
Players take turns to pick up a card.

The first player to have in their hand **three** cards that add up to 1 or 2 wins the round. They get one point.

The first person to win 10 points wins the game.

## B **Two decimal places** (p 127)

◊ As before, the teacher-led introduction should include discussion of mental and written methods. The weights of cheese can be used for this and some examples of suitable questions are shown below.

• How much do the two pieces of cheese weigh in total?

• How much heavier is the Cheddar than the Brie?

• What would be the weight of three pieces of Brie like this?

• What would be the weight of two pieces of Cheddar like this?

• If the Brie was cut into four equal pieces, how heavy would each piece be?

• If the Cheddar was cut into three equal pieces, how heavy would each piece be?

Include mental work such as

- $1.49 + 0.51$
- $1.35 - 0.9$
- $23.78 + 0.01$
- $169.31 - 0.1$
- $0.04 \times 9$

As before, include work on standard column procedures.

## C **Multiplying and dividing by 10, 100, 1000, ...** (p 130)

## D **Metric units** (p 131)

Use the table to discuss how to convert metric quantities for weight and length, bringing out when to multiply and when to divide.

## E **Buying food** (p 132)

Some questions involve rounding to the nearest penny.

◊ The information on the pupil's page can be used as the basis for some mental work such as 'What is the cost of 2 kg of pepperoni?'

Move on to problems such as 'What is the cost of 1.8 kg of pepperoni?' where pupils understand that they need to find £14.05 × 1.8 to find the total cost.

Include problems such as 'What is the cost of 1.6 kg of Cheddar?' that involve rounding to the nearest penny.

◊ Emphasise that:
  • The cost of, say, 1.6 kg of cheddar lies between the cost of 1 kg and the cost of 2 kg.
  • The cost of, say, 0.8 kg is less than the cost of a kilogram. (Multiplication by a number between 0 and 1 reduces.)

## F Unit cost (p 133)

◊ Encourage pupils who are not sure whether to multiply or divide (and also which way round to divide) to try the problem with 'easier' numbers. For example, if 2 kg of ham cost £10, how could you work out how much 1 kg of ham would cost?

Encourage pupils to check whether their answers seem sensible.

## G Mixed questions (p 134)

## A One decimal place (p 125)

**A1** (a) 7.2 (b) 4 (c) 3.9 (d) 4.1
(e) 11.2 (f) 2.5 (g) 6.1 (h) 1.9
(i) 0.9 (j) 1.5

**A2** (a) 3.6 (b) 6 (c) 5.4 (d) 16
(e) 5.2 (f) 0.5 (g) 2.4 (h) 1.6
(i) 0.4 (j) 1.5

**A3** (a) Cheddar: 1.2 kg   Stilton: 0.9 kg
(b) 0.3 kg (c) 2.1 kg (d) 6 kg
(e) 1.8 kg (f) 0.3 kg (g) 0.3 kg

**A4** B, C, D and E are wrong.
B: 6.2 × 9 = 55.8   C: 12.8 ÷ 8 = 1.6
D: 3.3 × 5 = 16.5   E: 17 − 6.8 = 10.2

**A5** (a) 17.2 (b) 3.5 (c) 16.8
(d) 2.5 (e) 30.1 (f) 51.8
(g) 2.6 (h) 31.2 (i) 3
(j) 6.3 (k) 0.4 (l) 2.4
(m) 10.2 (n) 16.8 (o) 2.2
(p) 8.5

**A6** The pupil's two weights that add to 3.1 kg

**A7** 7.5 litres

**A8** 20.8 metres

**A9** 1.4 metres

**A10** 0.2 litres

**A11** 9.5 kg

**A12** 28.4 × 7 = 198.8 kg
so the truck can carry all the boxes.

**A13** (a) 14.4 − 3.6
(b) (i) 7.2 ÷ 6
(ii) 0.9 × 3 or 1.2 + 1.5
(iii) 0.8 + 1.5
(iv) 14.4 ÷ 3
(c) 7.2 ÷ 3, 1.2 × 2, 6 − 3.6, 0.8 × 3, 14.4 ÷ 6, 0.9 + 1.5

## B Two decimal places (p 127)

**B1** (a) 1.65    (b) 13.79    (c) 6.03
    (d) 127.96    (e) 2    (f) 2.6
    (g) 13.95    (h) 2.55    (i) 7.2
    (j) 0.05    (k) 0.24    (l) 5.62

**B2** (a) 0.1    (b) 0.3    (c) 0.01
    (d) 5    (e) 18.92    (f) 7.45

**B3** A and D are wrong.
    A: $2.32 + 4.9 = 7.22$   D: $6.54 - 3.9 = 2.64$

**B4** (a) 10.13    (b) 12.51    (c) 869.35
    (d) 1.93    (e) 118.47    (f) 1.32
    (g) 4.37    (h) 116.04

**B5**

(a)
$$\begin{array}{r} 5.34 \\ + 16.76 \\ \hline 22.10 \end{array}$$

(b)
$$\begin{array}{r} 6.71 \\ - 0.23 \\ \hline 6.48 \end{array}$$

(c)
$$\begin{array}{r} 5.02 \\ - 1.61 \\ \hline 3.41 \end{array}$$

(d)
$$\begin{array}{r} 123.50 \\ - 17.32 \\ \hline 106.18 \end{array}$$

**B6** (a) 29.14    (b) 495.01

**B7** (a) 0.05    (b) 6.03    (c) 0.24
    (d) 0.52    (e) 0.56

**B8** (a) 9.12    (b) 31.2    (c) 63.18
    (d) 31.34    (e) 2470.08

**B9**

(a)
$$\begin{array}{r} 12.36 \\ \times \quad 4 \\ \hline 49.44 \end{array}$$

(b)
$$\begin{array}{r} 15.06 \\ \times \quad 3 \\ \hline 45.18 \end{array}$$

(c)
$$\begin{array}{r} 0.56 \\ \times \quad 9 \\ \hline 5.04 \end{array}$$

(d)
$$\begin{array}{r} 60.92 \\ \times \quad 8 \\ \hline 487.36 \end{array}$$

**B10** (a) 1.34    (b) 4.84    (c) 5.91
    (d) 0.21    (e) 7.22

**B11** The pupil's explanation

**B12** (a) $6.6 \div 4 = 1.65$
    (b) $18.36 \div 9 = 2.04$
    (c) $6.21 \times 5 = 31.05$
    (d) $3.1 \div 5 = 0.62$

**B13** (a) 2.65    (b) 3.58    (c) 2.45
    (d) 3.05    (e) 4.62

**B14** (a) 6.19 m    (b) 0.03 m
    (c) 15.2 m    (d) 2.32 m

**B15** (a) $6 \div 4$
    (b) (i) $2 - 1.2$    (ii) $6 \div 8$
       (iii) $23.2 \div 4$    (iv) $5.44 \times 3$
       (v) $2.4 \div 5$
    (c) $23.2 \times 3 = 69.6$
    (d) $2 \div 8 = 0.25$

**\*B16** (a) (i) $18.8 \to \div 5 \to - 1.2 \to \div 4 \to 0.64$
       (ii) $18.8 \to \div 4 \to - 1.2 \to \div 5 \to 0.7$
       (iii) $18.8 \to - 1.2 \to \div 4 \to \div 5 \to 0.88$
          or $18.8 \to - 1.2 \to \div 5 \to \div 4 \to 0.88$
    (b) (i) $5.44 \to - 1.2 \to \div 4 \to + 3.6 \to 4.66$
       (ii) $5.44 \to + 3.6 \to \div 4 \to - 1.2 \to 1.06$

## C Multiplying and dividing by 10, 100, 1000, ... (p 130)

**C1** (a) 471    (b) 0.471    (c) 383
    (d) 4920    (e) 2.68    (f) 0.157
    (g) 10    (h) 0.074    (i) 71
    (j) 0.9    (k) 30    (l) 0.012

**C2** (a) 100    (b) 45    (c) 2.1
    (d) 100    (e) 1.54    (f) 12
    (g) 1000    (h) 10    (i) 0.8

**C3** (a) 3.2 **320 32 0.32**
    (b) 0.6 **600 6 0.06**
    (c) 56 **0.056 0.0056 0.56**
    (d) **4.23** 423 **4.23 0.0423**
    (e) **30.9 0.309** 3.09 **0.00309**

## D Metric units (p 131)

**D1** (a) B: $4.2 \times 1000$    (b) D: $4.2 \div 100$

**D2** (a) 1234 g    (b) 2450 g    (c) 1500 g
    (d) 800 g    (e) 60 g

**D3** (a) 23.9 km    (b) 124.8 km    (c) 0.56 km
    (d) 9.2 km    (e) 0.09 km

**D4** (a) 7.8 cm    (b) 78 cm    (c) 0.2 cm
     (d) 4510 cm    (e) 9.8 cm

**D5** (a) 0.6 m    (b) 2350 m    (c) 4.9 m
     (d) 90 m      (e) 56.7 m

**D6** 67 g, 0.07 kg, 300 g, 0.5 kg, 892 g,
     0.985 kg, 1.04 kg

**D7** (a) 6000 ml      (b) 3612 ml
     (c) 15 200 ml      (d) 8070 ml
     (e) 20 ml

**D8** (a) 4.765 l    (b) 6.7 l      (c) 0.9 l
     (d) 0.042 l    (e) 0.007 l

**D9** 250 ml

**D10** 7.5 kg

**D11** 195 cm

**D12** 40 days

**D13** 2500 days

### E Buying food (p 132)

**E1** (a) 2.3 kg is heavier than 2 kg and
       2 kg of olives cost £13.00.
     (b) £14.95

**E2** (a) 0.8 kg is lighter than 1 kg and
       1 kg of pepperoni costs £14.05.
     (b) £11.24

**E3** (a) £36.53    (b) £6.53    (c) £2.04
     (d) £9.92     (e) £3.31    (f) £21.08
     (g) £17.04    (h) £3.26    (i) £11.41
     (j) £11.30    (k) £7.35    (l) £7.45

### F Unit cost (p 133)

**F1** (a) £0.57    (b) £0.60    (c) £0.65

**F2** £2.30

**F3** (a) £0.77 per litre (b) £0.73 per litre
     (c) £2.51 per kg   (d) £1.52 per metre
     (e) £0.87 per kg    (f) £0.44 per litre
     (g) £0.94 per kg   (h) £1.15 per kg

**F4** (a) Pack B
     (b) Pack A rose food costs £1.67 per kg.
       Pack B rose food costs £1.33 per kg.

**F5** (a) Box of 5: cost per pie £0.21
       Box of 8: cost per pie £0.24
       The box of 5 gives more for your
       money.
     (b) Box of 6: cost per egg £0.18
       Box of 10: cost per egg £0.17
       The box of 10 gives more for your
       money.
     (c) 2.5 kg bag: cost per kg £1.30
       1.5 kg bag: cost per kg £1.23
       The 1.5 kg bag gives more for your
       money.
     (d) 3.2 kg bag: cost per kg £0.66
       4.5 kg bag: cost per kg £0.59
       The 4.5 kg bag gives more for your
       money.
     (e) 8 metre roll: cost per m 12p
       15 metre roll: cost per m 11p
       The 15 metre roll gives more for
       your money.
     (f) 200 ml carton: cost per ml = 0.18p
       250 ml carton: cost per ml = 0.196p
       The 200 ml carton gives more for
       your money.

### G Mixed questions (p 134)

**G1** (a) £2.91    (b) £4.03    (c) 24p

**G2** £5.52

**G3** £1.05

**G4** £2.45

**G5** £3.71

**G6** £8.48

**G7** (a) £5.98        (b) £3.18
     (c) (i) £0.27    (ii) £0.26    (iii) £0.25

**G8** (a) A: £2.30, B: £1.59, C: £1.50
     (b) Can C      (c) £11.50
     (d) £3.55      (e) £0.95

**What progress have you made?** (p 135)

1  (a)  6.1      (b)  5.7      (c)  240
   (d)  2.31     (e)  4.5      (f)  18
   (g)  5.6      (h)  0.7      (i)  0.45

2  (a)  35.51    (b)  10.77    (c)  7.12
   (d)  101.2    (e)  4.06     (f)  6.94

3  (a)  0.56 kg          (b)  340 cm

4  £2.33

5  £2.15 per kg

## Practice booklet

## Section A (p 52)

1  1.1 litres

2  (a)  0.6 kg          (b)  4.4 kg

3  (a)  7.7            (b)  4.3
   (c)  3.9            (d)  18.7
   (e)  1.2            (f)  2
   (g)  7.2            (h)  5.5
   (i)  23.7           (j)  10
   (k)  201.9          (l)  11

4  (a)  6.1      (b)  7        (c)  5.9
   (d)  2.5      (e)  0.4      (f)  3.4
   (g)  0.3      (h)  2.8      (i)  8.3
   (j)  151.3    (k)  14.5     (l)  0.5

5  (a)  0.1 and 0.8  or  0.2 and 0.7
   (b)  0.9 and 0.5
   (c)  0.1 and 0.9  or  0.2 and 0.8
        or  0.3 and 0.7
   (d)  0.8, 0.9 and 0.7
   (e)  0.8, 0.5 and 0.7  or  0.8, 0.9 and 0.3
   (f)  0.2, 0.1 and 0.7  or  0.2, 0.5 and 0.3
   (g)  0.2, 0.1, 0.8, 0.9, 0.3 and 0.7
        or  0.1, 0.8, 0.9, 0.5 and 0.7

6  6 kg

7  4.2 kg

8  (a)  6.8      (b)  5.4      (c)  11.2
   (d)  10       (e)  0.4      (f)  36.5
   (g)  1.8      (h)  2.1      (i)  14.4
   (j)  12.6     (k)  4.5      (l)  36.4
   (m) 3         (n)  51.2     (o)  5.4
   (p)  56.7

9  20.4 metres

10  6.3 metres

11  (a)  1.4      (b)  1.6      (c)  2.8
    (d)  3.2      (e)  0.6      (f)  3.5
    (g)  10.7     (h)  0.7      (i)  5.7
    (j)  5.4      (k)  9.3      (l)  2.2
    (m) 101.9     (n)  20.3     (o)  95.4
    (p)  41.5

12  3.9 cm

13  0.3 litres

14  $8 \times 46.2 = 369.6$ which is less than 370 so
    the lift can carry all the boxes.

15  2.2 pounds

## Section B (p 55)

1  (a)  11.13    (b)  6.25     (c)  15.73
   (d)  21.26    (e)  43.09    (f)  204.21

2  (a)  1.73     (b)  1.58     (c)  180.55
   (d)  1.24     (e)  23.86    (f)  246.97
   (g)  1.04     (h)  7.49     (i)  331.03

3  (a)  3.28     (b)  6.57     (c)  26.12
   (d)  12.45    (e)  21.06    (f)  183.05
   (g)  5628.88  (h)  28.08    (i)  951.05

4  (a)  1.71     (b)  12.82    (c)  37.79
   (d)  1.68     (e)  2.04     (f)  6.14
   (g)  1.35     (h)  3.45     (i)  47.25

5  0.85 metres

6  1.56 metres

7  8.75 kg

**8** 0.06 metres or 6 centimetres

**9** £10.30

**10** £2.90

**11** £12.10

**12** £1.95

**13** £0.85

**14** £1.95

**15** £10.15

**16** 0.25 litres

**17** £2.37

## Section C (p 57)

**1** (a) 740    (b) 7.4    (c) 740

    (d) 7.4    (e) 740    (f) 0.74

**2** (a) 500    (b) 12    (c) 5.7

    (d) 35.4    (e) 3    (f) 2.32

    (g) 7684    (h) 2.43    (i) 0.345

    (j) 250    (k) 3450    (l) 0.81

    (m) 1249    (n) 6.426    (o) 23

    (p) 8.325    (q) 5020    (r) 0.037

    (s) 62.3    (t) 0.08    (u) 10

    (v) 150    (w) 20.05    (x) 0.00034

**3** (a) 100    (b) 10    (c) 6.2

    (d) 100    (e) 26    (f) 100

    (g) 1000    (h) 1.2    (i) 0.000342

## Section D (p 58)

**1** (a) 671 grams    (b) 1230 grams

    (c) 500 grams    (d) 3 grams

**2** (a) 8.035 litres    (b) 0.5 litres

    (c) 0.839 litres    (d) 0.06 litres

**3** (a) 4.3 cm    (b) 167 cm

    (c) 0.5 cm    (d) 320 cm

**4** (a) 6300 m    (b) 60 m

    (c) 4.23 m    (d) 0.3 m

**5** 1.2 litres, 1.08 litres, 0.5 litres, 450 ml, 2.3 ml

## Section E (p 58)

**1** (a) £1.96    (b) £1.30    (c) £0.63

    (d) £0.94    (e) £1.72    (f) £0.68

    (g) £0.70    (h) £0.23    (i) £0.47

    (j) £0.83

## Section F (p 59)

**1** In the 1 litre bottle, 1 litre costs £3.75. In the $1\frac{1}{2}$ litre bottle 1 litre costs £3.97. In the 2 litre bottle, 1 litre costs £3.98.

The 1 litre bottle gives most for your money.

**2** The 1.8 kg piece costs £2.59 per kilo. The 1.3 kg piece costs £2.37 per kilo.

The 1.3 kg piece is the better deal.

**3** (In these answers, the first unit cost is for the first item and answers are given correct to the nearest penny.)

    (a) 87p/litre; 75p/litre; the 2 litre bottle is better

    (b) 18p/roll; 19p/roll; the 12 rolls are better

    (c) 17p/cracker; 18p/cracker; the box of 12 is better

    (d) 30p/kg; 31p/kg; the 5 kg is better

    (e) £1.17/kg; £1.15/kg; the 20 kg is better

    (f) £1.56/metre; £1.60/metre; the 24 metres is better

    (g) 65p/kg; 51p/kg; the 2.5 kg is better

    (h) 49p/ litre; 48p/litre; the 12.5 litres is better

    (i) £1.47/kg; £1.54/kg; the 3.1 kg is better

    (j) £1.33/kg; £1.33/kg; they cost the same per kilogram

    (k) £3.00/kg; £3.99/kg; the 2.5 kg bag is better

(l)   36p/kg;  37p/kg;
      the 2.5 kg is better
(m) 15p/cane;  13p/cane;
      the 105 canes are better
(n)  £3 750 000/mile;  £3 448 275.86/mile;
      the 2.9 miles is better

## Section G (p 60)

1  (a)  £1.72      (b)  £4.54      (c)  £1.34
   (d)  £2.52      (e)  £0.72      (f)  £2.36
   (g)  £3.44      (h)  £2.83

2  £6.92

3  (a)  £0.59      (b)  £1.13

4  (a)  £0.84      (b)  £0.29

5  £7.90

6  £0.25

7  £0.43

8  (a)  A: £2.22,  B: £2.00,  C: £1.11
   (b)  Bag C

9  (a)  A: £2.08,  B: £1.33,  C: £1.18
   (b)  6 kg bag: £1.40    25 kg bag: £1.05
   (c)  25 kg bag from the catalogue

# ⑲ Three dimensions

| Essential | Optional |
|---|---|
| Multilink cubes, triangular dotty paper | Sheet 170 |
| **Practice booklet** pages 62 to 64 | |

## Ⓐ Describing three-dimensional objects (p 136)

> Multilink cubes (about 10 for each pair of pupils)

◊ The aim is to promote visualisation of three-dimensional shapes and the language needed to describe them.

The partner making the model from the description will almost certainly want to seek clarification and ask further questions. This can help pupils describe the shapes more precisely.

## Ⓑ Drawing three-dimensional objects (p 136)

> Multilink cubes (about 6 per pupil), triangular dotty paper

## Ⓒ Views (p 137)

The choice of 'front' and 'side' view is arbitrary.

## Ⓓ Nets (p 139)

> Optional: Sheet 170

◊ Pupils should be encouraged to do as much as they can by visualising the three-dimensional shapes: they should cut out and fold nets only when they cannot visualise the shapes, or to check their thinking.

◊ Nets P, Q and R are on the optional resource sheet 170. Having discussed their sketches, perhaps first in small groups and then as a whole class, pupils could make the solids.

◊ P  square based pyramid    Q  cube with corner sliced off    R  'house' or cube with triangular prism

◊ Useful discussion questions are 'What is the same about the solid? What is different?' It is hoped that pupils will consider and discuss faces, vertices and edges, but do not force this.

## Ⓔ Surface area (p 141)

## B Drawing three-dimensional objects
(p 136)

**B1** The pupil's drawing

**B2** (a), (b), (c) The pupil's drawings

   (d)  T: 7   H: 11   E: 8

**B3** If shapes that are 'mirror images' of each other are counted as different, 8 shapes can be made with four cubes.

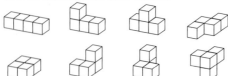

mirror images

**B4** The pupil's drawings

## C Views (p 137)

**C1** (a) 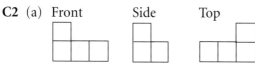   (b)

**C2** (a)  Front   Side   Top

   (b)  Front   Side   Top

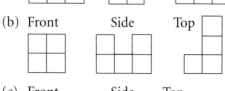

   (c)  Front   Side   Top

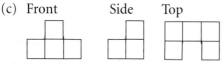

**C3** (a)  A P, B R, C S, D Q

   (b)  View from T

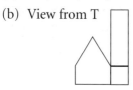

**C4** Mug  A, G

Spoon  B, D

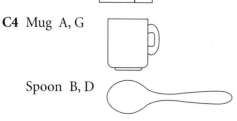

Toilet roll  C, E

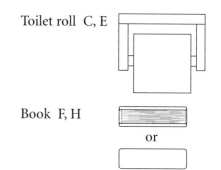

Book  F, H

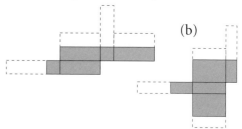

or

## D Nets (p 139)

**D1** (a)  Could        (b)  Could not

   (c)  Could not    (d)  Could

   (e)  Could

**D2** (a)  The missing face could go on the net in any one of four positions.

   (b)

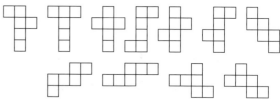

**D3** (a)  P and Q are nets of a cube, R is not.

   (b)  The arrangements which make a cube are

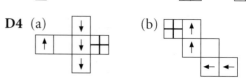

**D4** (a) 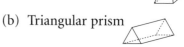   (b)

**D5** (a)  Square based pyramid

   (b)  Triangular prism

   (c)  Tetrahedron

(d) Triangular prism ('wedge')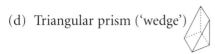

(e) Hexagonal prism

**D6** (a) There are several possibilities. Here are two.

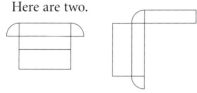

(b) There are several possibilities. Here is one.

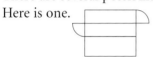

**D7** This is one of several possibilities.

E **Surface area** (p 141)

**E1** 126 cm$^2$

**E2** 100 cm$^2$

**E3** (a) 52 cm$^2$ (b) 122 cm$^2$
(c) 202 cm$^2$ (d) 158 cm$^2$

*E4 9 cm

**What progress have you made?** (p 141)

**1** The pupil's model and drawings

**2** This is one of several possibilities.

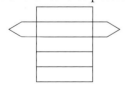

**3** 76 cm$^2$

**Practice booklet**

**Sections B and C** (p 62)

**1** (a)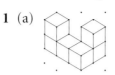

(b) (c) (d)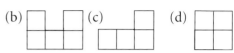

**2** front side top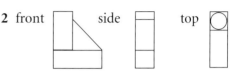

**3** A B C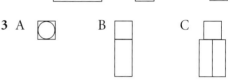

**Section D** (p 63)

**1** (a) (b) (c) (d)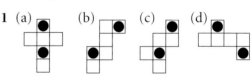

**2** There are two different possible dice, one with the numbers 2 3 5 4 going clockwise around the number 1,

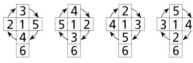

and the other with the numbers 2 3 5 4 going anticlockwise around the number 1.

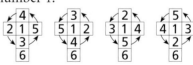

**3** B, E, F

**Section E** (p 64)

**1** (a) 14 cm (b) 84 cm$^2$ (c) 104 cm$^2$

**2** (a) 188 cm$^2$ (b) 136 cm$^2$ (c) 102 cm$^2$

**3** 7 cm

**4** 72 cm$^2$ (there are 18 squares)

# 20 Percentage

This unit covers changing a percentage to a decimal, calculating a percentage of a quantity and expressing one quantity as a percentage of another. The latter leads on to drawing pie charts using a circular percentage scale.

---

**Essential**

Pie chart scale

**Practice booklet** pages 65 to 69

---

## A Understanding percentages (p 142)

◊ Proportions are given in a variety of ways. From class or group discussion should emerge the need for a 'common currency' for expressing and comparing proportions.

◊ French cheeses may be labelled '40% matière grasse', for example; this means 40% of the dry matter is fat (i.e. the water content of the cheese is discounted).

◊ The order is:
Mascarpone 45%, Blue Stilton 36%, Red Leicester $33\frac{1}{3}$%, Danish Blue 28%, Edam 25%, Camembert 21%, Cottage Cheese 2%.

## B Percentages in your head (p 144)

Mental work with percentages can be returned to frequently in oral sessions.

## C Percentages and decimals (p 145)

## D Calculating a percentage of a quantity (p 147)

It is important that pupils should feel confident about their method of working out a percentage of a quantity. The 'one-step' method, treating the percentage as a decimal, is more sophisticated but ultimately better because it easily extends to a succession of percentage changes. It is used in section F.

## E Changing fractions to decimals (p 148)

You could point out that the division symbol ÷ is itself a fraction line with blanks above and below for numbers.

## F One number as a percentage of another (p 149)

The approach used here depends on conversion from decimal to percentage.

## G Drawing pie charts (p 151)

Pie chart scale

◊ The pie charts shown are not labelled with the percentages, in order to give practice in measuring. However, it is a good practice to show the percentages.

◊ Rounding often leads to percentages which add up to slightly more or less than 100%. For this reason, when drawing pie charts it is often better to work to the nearest 0.1% as the small excess or deficit can be safely ignored.

## A Understanding percentages (p 142)

**A1** (a) About 27%  (b) Water
  (c) About 21%

**A2** (a) C, D, F  (b) G, H
  (c) A, E  (d) B, I

**A3** (a) 20%–30%  (b) 85%–95%
  (c) 45%–55%  (d) 55%–65%
  (e) 3%–8%  (f) 65%–75%

## B Percentages in your head (p 144)

**B1** (a) $\frac{1}{4}$  (b) $\frac{3}{4}$  (c) $\frac{1}{10}$
  (d) $\frac{9}{10}$  (e) $\frac{1}{5}$

**B2** (a) 50%  (b) 10%  (c) 25%
  (d) 75%  (e) $33\frac{1}{3}$%, 25%

**B3** 37%

**B4** 72%

**B5** (a) £15  (b) £42  (c) £17.50

**B6** (a) £10  (b) £21  (c) £17.50

**B7** (a) To find 10%, you can divide by 10, giving 6 and 6.5.

(b) To find 5%, you can divide by 10, then halve.

**B8** (a) 1p  (b) 3p  (c) 37p

**B9** (a) 7p  (b) 21p

## C Percentages and decimals (p 145)

**C1** (a) 0.5  (b) 0.25  (c) 0.65
  (d) 0.78  (e) 0.1  (f) 0.01
  (g) 0.04  (h) 0.4

**C2** (a) 30%  (b) 80%  (c) 83%
  (d) 3%

**C3**

| Fraction | | Decimal | | Percentage |
|---|---|---|---|---|
| $\frac{70}{100}$ | = | **0.7** | = | **70%** |
| $\frac{45}{100}$ | = | **0.45** | = | **45%** |
| $\frac{57}{100}$ | = | 0.57 | = | **57%** |
| $\frac{85}{100}$ | = | 0.85 | = | **85%** |
| $\frac{5}{100}$ | = | **0.05** | = | **5%** |
| $\frac{63}{100}$ | = | **0.63** | = | 63% |
| $\frac{7}{100}$ | = | 0.07 | = | **7%** |

**C4** (a) 0.44    (b) 0.26    (c) 0.9

     (d) 0.84    (e) 0.55    (f) 0.05

     (g) 0.11    (h) 0.01    (i) 0.73

     (j) 0.2     (k) 0.06    (l) 0.19

**C5** (a) 72%    (b) 31%    (c) 50%

     (d) 1%     (e) 13%    (f) 40%

     (g) 2%     (h) 92%    (i) 4%

     (j) 85%    (k) 14%    (l) 56%

**C6** 1%, 0.1, $\frac{12}{100}$, 15%, 0.25, 0.3, $\frac{45}{100}$

**C7** $\frac{78}{100}$, 0.75, 65%, 0.51, 0.4, 0.08, 5%

**C8** (a) (i) $\frac{30}{100}$ (ii) 30%

     (b) (i) $\frac{40}{100}$ (ii) 40%

     (c) (i) $\frac{70}{100}$ (ii) 70%

     (d) (i) $\frac{20}{100}$ (ii) 20%

     (e) (i) $\frac{60}{100}$ (ii) 60%

     (f) (i) $\frac{15}{100}$ (ii) 15%

     (g) (i) $\frac{65}{100}$ (ii) 65%

     (h) (i) $\frac{35}{100}$ (ii) 35%

**C9** 0.08, $\frac{1}{10}$, 15%, 0.2, 0.56, 74%, $\frac{3}{4}$

## Ⓓ Calculating a percentage of a quantity (p 147)

**D1** (a) 162 g    (b) 256.2 g    (c) 66.7 g

     (d) 93.8 g    (e) 26.6 g    (f) 35.2 g

     (g) 201.6 g    (h) 52.8 g

**D2** (a) 2.25 g       (b) 6.72 g

     (c) 3.6 g        (d) 1.68 g

**D3** 410 g

**D4** 0.6 g

**D5** He is right for 10%, but dividing by 5 gives 20%, not 5%.

**D6** (a) Sugar 19.95 g, fat 10.5 g, protein 2.8 g

     (b) Sugar 85.5 g, fat 45 g, protein 12 g

     (c) Sugar 285 g, fat 150 g, protein 40 g

## Ⓔ Changing fractions to decimals (p 148)

**E1** (a) 0.25    (b) 0.125    (c) 0.05

     (d) 0.8     (e) 0.375    (f) 0.875

     (g) 0.28    (h) 0.15    (i) 0.22

     (j) 0.9375

**E2** $\frac{29}{50}$ (0.58), $\frac{3}{5}$ (0.6), $\frac{5}{8}$ (0.625), $\frac{13}{20}$ (0.65)

**E3** $\frac{17}{20}$ (0.85), $\frac{39}{50}$ (0.78), $\frac{19}{25}$ (0.76), $\frac{3}{4}$ (0.75)

**E4** (a) 0.14    (b) 0.57    (c) 0.11

     (d) 0.56    (e) 0.64    (f) 0.27

     (g) 0.08    (h) 0.38    (i) 0.41

     (j) 0.87

## Ⓕ One number as a percentage of another (p 149)

**F1** (a) $\frac{5}{7}$    (b) 71% (to the nearest 1%)

**F2** (a) 60%    (b) 35%    (c) 87.5%

     (d) about 33%    (e) about 67%

**F3** (a) 29%    (b) 78%    (c) 23%

     (d) 41%    (e) 5%

**F4** (a) $\frac{1}{4}$     (b) 25%    (c) 19%

**F5** (a) 30%    (b) 70%

**F6** (a) 86%    (b) 14%

**F7** 30%

**F8** Peter attended 83% of the practices. Carol attended 78% of the practices. So Peter has the better record.

**F9** (a) Model A (3% faulty)

     (b) Model D (14% faulty)

**\*F10** (a) 16%

     (b) In a class of 30 it would be about 5 people.

## Ⓖ Drawing pie charts (p 151)

**G1** These features (among others) may be noticed: Cheese spread has higher proportions of water and carbohydrate, but lower proportions of fat and protein.

**G2** (a) 28% (b) 23% (c) 46% (d) 53%

**G3**

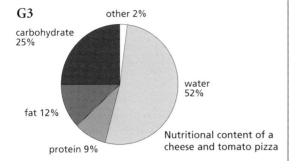

other 2%
carbohydrate 25%
water 52%
fat 12%
protein 9%
Nutritional content of a cheese and tomato pizza

**G4** (a) Meat, fish and eggs (b) 9%

(c) Clio is wrong. The chart shows money spent, not the amounts eaten.

**G5**

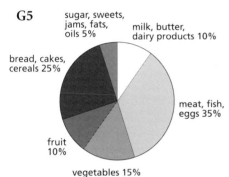

sugar, sweets, jams, fats, oils 5%
milk, butter, dairy products 10%
bread, cakes, cereals 25%
meat, fish, eggs 35%
fruit 10%
vegetables 15%

**G6** (a) 32 pages (b) 34%

(c) Foreign news 22%, sport 16%, entertainment 9%, finance 19%

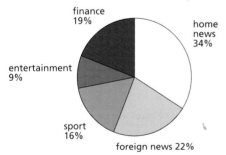

finance 19%
home news 34%
entertainment 9%
sport 16%
foreign news 22%

**G7**

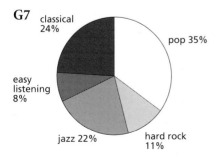

classical 24%
pop 35%
easy listening 8%
jazz 22%
hard rock 11%

## What progress have you made? (p 153)

1 (a) C (b) A (c) E

2 (a) 0.5 (b) 0.45 (c) 0.04 (d) 0.07

3 (a) £5 (b) 2 kg (c) 9 kg (d) £2

4 (a) 68.4 g (b) 13 g

5 73%

6 21 out of 25 (84%) is better than 30 out of 37 (81%).

7

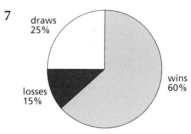

draws 25%
wins 60%
losses 15%

## Practice booklet

### Section A (p 65)

1 Cadbury's Double Decker:
protein 6%, fat 22%, carbohydrate 72%

Sainsbury's Creamy White:
protein 7%, fat 35%, carbohydrate 58%

2 (a) 30% (b) 10% (c) 70% (d) 50%

### Section B (p 66)

1 (a) £10 (b) £8.50 (c) £45

2 (a) £15 (b) £13 (c) £12.50

3 (a) 7 kg (b) £7.50 (c) £7.30

4 (a) 5p (b) 15p (c) £4.85
(d) 90p (e) £4.50

5 (a) Divide by 10 to find 10%.
(b) Divide by 10, then halve to get 5%.
(c) Add the results for 10% and 5% together.

6 (a) £1.50 (b) £6 (c) £13.50

7 (a) 3% of £10 is £0.30. Others are £3.

(b) 75% of £8 is £6. Others are £5.

(c) 5% of £80 is £4. Others are £4.50.

8 (a) £240    (b) £400    (c) £292

## Section C (p 67)

1 (a) 0.68    (b) 0.41    (c) 0.8

(d) 0.08    (e) 0.09    (f) 0.9

(g) 0.54    (h) 0.3

2 (a) 65%    (b) 60%    (c) 6%

(d) 7%    (e) 2%    (f) 22%

(g) 20%    (h) 3%

3

| | | | | |
|---|---|---|---|---|
| $\frac{58}{100}$ | = | **0.58** | = | **58%** |
| $\frac{32}{100}$ | = | 0.32 | = | **32%** |
| $\frac{9}{100}$ | = | **0.09** | = | **9%** |
| $\frac{80}{100}$ | = | **0.8** | = | 80% |
| $\frac{5}{100}$ | = | 0.05 | = | **5%** |

4 (a) 7%    $\frac{8}{100}$    0.09    0.1    0.8    $\frac{81}{100}$

(b) 0.02    0.1    12%    20%    $\frac{1}{2}$    0.7

(c) 0.07    $\frac{8}{100}$    0.3 and $\frac{3}{10}$    40%    75%

## Section D (p 67)

1 28% of 4 = 1.12    47% of 220 = 103.4
91% of 7.3 = 6.643   8% of 8 = 0.64
The extra calculation is 26% of 82 = 21.32

2 A is the odd one out (£10). Others are £6.

3 A is the odd one out (3.2 kg).
Others are 3.3 kg.

4 (a) £1275    (b) £7225

5 (a) £410    (b) £36 306    (c) £2856

## Sections E and F (p 68)

1 (a) $\frac{6}{11}$ = 55%, $\frac{11}{19}$ = 58%, $\frac{13}{27}$ = 48%

(b) $\frac{13}{27}$, $\frac{6}{11}$, $\frac{11}{19}$

2 76%

3 12%

4 (a) 31%    (b) 69%

5 (a) Screen 3 (87%)

(b) Screen 2 (37%)

6 (a) 8.7%    (b) 88.4%    (c) 2.9%

## Section G (p 69)

1 The proportion working in agriculture is the same in both places.
A bigger proportion are working in service industries and in distribution and catering in Latin America.
A bigger proportion are working in manufacturing, construction and transport and communications in Eastern Europe.

2 (a), (b)

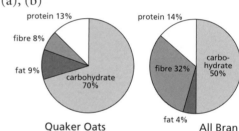

Quaker Oats          All Bran

(c) The protein content of each are similar, but All Bran contains a lot more fibre and less carbohydrate and fat than Quaker Oats.

3 (a), (b)

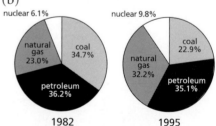

1982          1995

(b) The use of coal has dropped considerably. Natural gas and nuclear energy have increased their shares.

# Review 3 (p 154)

1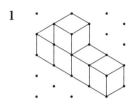

2 (a) 75%          (b) 25%

3 (a) 6.05 kg      (b) 0.45 kg

4 (a) 2 500 000 grams
  (b) 10 000

5 0.3 kg

6 86 cm

7 (a) £11.34       (b) £0.42 or 42p

8 Star

9 (a) D   (b) C   (c) A   (d) B

10 Phoebe    6.74 kg
   Hayley    7 kg
   Jennifer  7.04 kg
   Kate      8.1 kg

11 20 days

12 $\frac{1}{2}$      50%
   $\frac{1}{4}$      25%
   $\frac{1}{5}$      20%
   $\frac{3}{5}$      60%
   $\frac{3}{10}$     30%

13 (a) 0.34 kg      (b) 3.06 kg

14 23 days

15 £24

16 7.6 cm

17 B

18 0.03, $\frac{1}{4}$, 30%, 0.42, $\frac{4}{5}$, 90%

19 (a) 5928        (b) 6000

20 150 ml, 0.175 litres, 0.2 litres, 225 ml, 0.30 litres

21 (a) One correct net is
   (b) 284.1 cm²

5.3 cm
4.1 cm   12.8 cm

22 14.7 kg

23 (a) 13%
   (b) (i) 0.120 kg   (ii) 120 grams

## Mixed questions 3 (Practice booklet p 70)

1 The multiplications may be written in either order.
   (a) 0.4 × 3       (b) 0.4 × 8
   (c) 0.6 × 8       (d) 0.6 × 5
   (e) 0.1 × 8       (f) 0.6 × 3

2 (a)  0.8        (b)  1.5        (c)  1.4
       × 3             × 2             × 3
       2.4             3.0             4.2

   (d)  2.5        (e)  1.3        (f)  1.8
       × 3             × 4             × 3
       7.5             5.2             5.4

3 1.68 m

4 (a) 4.48        (b) 4.61        (c) 4.74
  (d) 4.87        (e) 5.04        (f) 9.91
  (g) 10.05       (h) 10.29       (i) 10.44

5 (a) 10 cm²   (b) 40 cm²   (c) 90 cm²
  (d) When the lengths in (a) are multiplied by a number, the surface area in (a) is multiplied by the square of that number.

6 (a) CAT           (b) GERBIL
  (c) HAMSTER       (d) GOLDFISH

7 69%

# Fair to all?

| Essential | Optional |
|---|---|
| Packs of playing cards or number cards (for 'Mean tricks') Newspapers/foreign language texts (for the investigation on page 163) | Sheet 171 |
| **Practice booklet** pages 72 to 75 | |

## 𝔸 **How to be fair** (p 157)

Decimal means occur in this section but no rounding is necessary.

> Optional: Sheet 171

◊ You could start by asking the class which group they think did better.

Ann's group collected 20 kg of paper, Ben's group collected 18 kg. However, there are more pupils in Ann's group, and pupils may argue that Ben's group collected 6 kg per pupil while Ann's group only managed 5 kg per pupil. Introduce the mean weight of newspapers as the result of sharing the newspaper equally between members of the group.

Sheet 171 can be used to illustrate this further.

Pupils should be aware that the existence of a mean value does not imply that such a value must exist in practice. For example, the mean for Ann's group is 5 kg and no one collected that amount.

You may wish to extend your initial discussion to include decimal means. For example, 'What if Ann collected 5 kg instead of 3 kg?'

◊ Decimal means first occur in question A7. You may wish pupils to try A1 to A6 without a calculator to consolidate number skills. Use of a calculator is assumed in all subsequent work.

**A7** This can generate discussion. Using means puts Wayne (8.5) at the top followed by Pat (8) and Jon (7.8). However, using medians puts Jon (8) at the top followed by Pat (7.5) and Wayne (6.5). Pupils may also bring in the idea of consistency.

## Mean tricks (p 160)

Pupils can practise their mental skills in calculating the mean for small data sets and the game also helps them consolidate the idea of the mean.

> Packs of playing cards (picture cards removed). Alternatively, sets of 40 number cards (four 1s, four 2s, four 3s etc.) could be used instead.

◊ Schools have found that the benefits of this game improve with playing as pupils develop strategies to calculate the mean quickly.

Suppose the target mean is 6. Some pupils may use the strategy of looking for two cards with a total of 12, three cards with a total of 18, four cards with a total of 24 and so on. Others may use a method where they try to make the total deviation from the mean zero. For example the total deviation of 5, 4, 6 and 9 from 6 is $^{-}1 + ^{-}2 + 0 + 3 = 0$ so the mean of this set must be 6. Pupils could compare their methods.

## B Means from frequencies (p 160)

Pupils need to be able to round to one or two decimal places.

◊ Show how the frequency table relates to the weights of the players in the football team. Pupils should be clear that, say, the first line of the table shows that there are 3 people that weigh 70 kg in the team.

Emphasise that pupils are to try to answer the questions just by looking at the numbers in the table. However, looking at the illustration above the table should help clarify things for pupils who find this difficult.

◊ It is worth spending time on the meaning of the word 'frequency' with respect to each question. It is a very common misconception to add up the frequencies and divide that by the number of frequencies that occur.

◊ Encourage pupils to lay out their work carefully. It may help them to add a 'total' column to each table and fill this in. The table on page 160 could be extended like this

| Weight in kg | Frequency | Total weight |
|--------------|-----------|--------------|
| 70 | 3 | 210 |
| 71 | 2 | 142 |
| 72 | 4 | 288 |
| 73 | 2 | 146 |

When working with frequency tables it can help trace a mistake if all steps are shown.

**B12** In part (c), watch out for pupils who try to find the mean age of the choir by finding the mean of the means found in parts (a) and (b), obtaining 13.625 years.

◊ An additional activity is to choose a book and try to estimate the number of words in the book. This is likely to involve estimating the mean number of words on a line and working from there. Pupils could also consider questions such as 'How many pages in the book would come to 5000 words?'

### Investigation (p 163)

> Newspapers and foreign language texts

◊ Pupils can of course compare any two papers; collated results make an interesting wall display. Samples should be of a reasonable size – counting the number of words in, say, 40 sentences and finding the mean using a frequency table would be fine.

This has been found to be a very useful homework task.

## ℂ Averages (p 164)

This section brings together the three measures of average – mean, median and mode – and introduces the idea of the most representative average.

◊ Discussion of the three initial statements should bring out that the word 'average' is used loosely to mean 'about the middle'.

In the statement 'Mary is of average height.' Is 'average height' the average for the school year? the school? the population of the UK?

What average could it be?

What average do you think is appropriate? Why?

The other statements can be discussed similarly.

◊ Pupils should think about which of the pocket money averages is a good representative average for this data. They are likely to find this idea quite difficult. They may see that the mode is not very representative as over half the young people receive £4.50 or more. Choosing between the mean and median is more difficult. Ask pupils if the median would change if the five pupils that received £3.00 or less actually all received £1.00. This may help them see that the median is unchanged by the relative poverty of these five! In this case the mean can be regarded as the most representative as there are no very large or small values to distort it.

◊ In questions C2 to C4, ordering the data can be tedious. Encourage pupils to think about how to record the results to make finding the averages easier, for example a dot plot or tally chart/frequency table.

## A How to be fair (p 157)

**A1** (a) 6 kg    (b) 7 kg    (c) Jason's group

**A2** $27 \div 9 = 3$

**A3** $120 \div 10 = 12$ goldfish

**A4** (a) $40 \div 5 = 8$ pupils

    (b) $36 \div 4 = 9$ pupils

**A5** $35 \div 5 = 7$ peppers per plant

**A6** Ruth is right: the 24 peppers have to be shared between the four plants.

**A7**  Pat      $32 \div 4$ or 8 points per game

      Jon      $39 \div 5$ or 7.8 points per game

      Wayne   $51 \div 6$ or 8.5 points per game

    You could argue that Wayne is the best points scorer as his mean number of points is the highest. However, it could also be argued that Pat's mean is only 0.5 less than Wayne's and she is more consistent that him.

**A8** (a) Means:  8L  $40 \div 20 = 2$ cans

                8N  $55 \div 25 = 2.2$ cans

    8N has a higher mean and you could argue from this that it should get the prize.

    (b) Means:  8L  $50 \div 20 = 2.5$ bottles

                8N  $60 \div 25 = 2.4$ bottles

    8L has a higher mean and you could argue from this that it should get the prize.

    (c) The pupil's view and explanation

    8L collected a mean of $90 \div 20 = 4.5$ items per person and 8N collected a mean of $115 \div 25 = 4.6$ items per person so you could argue that 8N did better overall.

**A9** Answers can be found by calculating the mean load pulled by a member of the team (although this assumes a similar level of fitness for each team member).

The mean loads pulled per person are:

Team A: $2475 \div 9 = 275$ kg

Team B: $1656 \div 6 = 276$ kg

Team C: $1911 \div 7 = 273$ kg

(a) Team B        (b) Team C

The pupil's reasons

## B Means from frequencies (p 160)

**B1** (a) 15 players

    (b) 5 players

    (c) $(75 \times 1) + (76 \times 4) + (77 \times 3) + (78 \times 5) + (79 \times 2) = 1158$ kg

    (d) $1158 \div 15 = 77.2$ kg

**B2** (a) 35 nests

    (b) $(3 \times 17) + (4 \times 15) + (5 \times 3) = 126$ eggs

    (c) $126 \div 35 = 3.6$ eggs

**B3** (a) 40 games

    (b) 23 games

    (c) $(0 \times 5) + (1 \times 12) + (2 \times 13) + (3 \times 8) + (4 \times 2) = 70$ goals

    (d) $70 \div 40 = 1.75$ goals

**B4** (a) 40 plants

    (b) $(4 \times 7) + (5 \times 9) + (6 \times 11) + (7 \times 10) + (8 \times 3) = 233$ tomatoes

    (c) $233 \div 40 = 5.8$ tomatoes (to 1 d.p.)

**B5** $(26 \times 2) + (28 \times 22) + (29 \times 13) + (30 \times 13) = 1435$ Smarties

$1435 \div 50 = 28.7$ Smarties

**B6** (a)

| Price | Frequency |
|-------|-----------|
| 57p | 3 |
| 58p | 5 |
| 59p | 5 |
| 60p | 3 |
| 61p | 4 |

    (b) $(57 \times 3) + (58 \times 5) + (59 \times 5) + (60 \times 3) + (61 \times 4) = 1180$p

    $1180 \div 20 = 59$p

**B7** 5.97 (to 2 d.p.) with the pupil's description

**B8** $(8 \times 2) + (7 \times 3) + (6 \times 9) + (5 \times 1) = 96$

$96 \div 15 = 6.4$ tomatoes

**B9** $(1 \times 40) + (2 \times 30) + (3 \times 18) + (4 \times 12) + (5 \times 4) = 222$ people
$222 \div 104 = 2.1$ people (to 1 d.p.)

**B10** (a) $(48 \times 10) + (49 \times 27) + (50 \times 39) + (51 \times 67) + (52 \times 34)$
$= 8938$ matches
$8938 \div 177 = 50.5$ matches
(to 1 d.p.)

(b) The statement seems fair. Although you might only get 48 matches, the mean is more than the 50 stated.

**B11** (a) The pupil's set of five numbers
(b) The mean increases by 2.
(c) The mean increases by the number you add to each of your set of numbers.
(d) $9760 + [(1 + 3 + 0 + 2 + 4) \div 5]$
$= 9762$

**B12** (a) $265 \div 20 = 13.25$ years
(b) $420 \div 30 = 14$ years
(c) $685 \div 50 = 13.7$ years

**B13** (a) 11.75 years   (b) 14 years

ℂ **Averages** (p 164)

**C1** (a) Median   (b) Mode

**C2** (a) £2.50   (b) £2.35
(c) £3.00   (d) Mode

**C3** (a) (i)  23 years
(ii)  $794 \div 30 = 26.5$ years (to 1 d.p.)
(iii) 18 years

(b) It could change at a day's notice, depending on when members' birthdays are. The frequencies are also too low for the mode to be relevant.

(c)

| Age | Frequency |
|---|---|
| 10–19 | 11 |
| 20–29 | 9 |
| 30–39 | 6 |
| 40–49 | 3 |
| 50–59 | 1 |

The modal age group is 10–19.

**C4** (a)

| Hours | Number of days (Blackmouth) | Number of days (Bournepool) |
|---|---|---|
| 1 | 2 | 3 |
| 2 | 1 | 1 |
| 3 | 3 | 2 |
| 4 | 5 | 4 |
| 5 | 5 | 3 |
| 6 | 2 | 2 |
| 7 | 1 | 7 |
| 8 | 3 | 6 |
| 9 | 4 | 3 |
| 10 | 3 | 0 |
| 11 | 2 | 0 |

*Blackmouth*
median: 5 hours
mean: $189 \div 31 = 6.1$ hours (to 1 d.p.)
modes: 4 and 5 hours

*Bournepool*
median: 7 hours
mean: $178 \div 31 = 5.7$ hours (to 1 d.p.)
mode: 7 hours
Although the mean number of hours of sunshine is less for Bournepool (5.7 compared with 6.1), the median is higher. This means that half the days at Bournepool have 7 or more hours of sunshine compared with 5 or more at Blackmouth. The mode of 7 hours at Bournepool is more than that of the two most frequent amounts of sunshine at Blackmouth (4 and 5 hours).

(b) The pupil's adverts

## Challenge

It can take some time to list them all, so you could just ask for what pupils can find.

There are 21 sets, some of which are listed here:
1, 2, 3, 5, 6, 18, 21   1, 2, 3, 5, 11, 13, 21
1, 2, 4, 5, 6, 17, 21   1, 3, 4, 5, 8, 14, 21
2, 3, 4, 5, 9, 11, 22

**What progress have you made?** (p 166)

**1** £37.24 ÷ 7 = £5.32

**2** (a)  Mean: 137 ÷ 30 = 4.6 hours (to 1 d.p.)
        Mode: 0 hours
        Median: 5 hours
    (b)  Median or mean. The mode of 0
        hours is not at all representative.

**3** 1155 ÷ 50 = 23.1 calculators

## Practice booklet

### Section A (p 72)

**1** 14 ÷ 7 = 2 hours

**2** Kathy did better.
    Her mean score was 3.5, higher than
    Mark's mean score of 3.4.

**3** (a)  The girls' mean pocket money is
        £40.00 ÷ 10 = £4.00
    (b)  The boys' mean pocket money is
        £31.60 ÷ 8 = £3.95

**4** 60 ÷ 15 = 4 letters per word

**5** 388 ÷ 8 = 48.5p

**6** (a)  The pupil's answer, for example
        5, 7, 9 or 3, 5, 13
    (b)  The total of the three numbers must
        be 21 which is an odd number.
        When even numbers are added the
        answer is always even.

**7** The pupil's answer (the total of the
    five numbers must be 47)

### Section B (p 73)

**1** (3 × 28) + (1 × 26) = 110
    110 ÷ 4 = 27.5 teeth

**2** (1 × 50) + (2 × 25) + (3 × 20) + (4 × 3) +
    (5 × 2) = 182
    182 ÷ 100 = 1.82 people

**3** (4 × 5) + (5 × 1) + ... + (14 × 4) = 460
    460 ÷ 50 = 9.2 eggs

### Section C (p 74)

**1** (a)  5410 ÷ 25 = 216.4 grams
    (b), (e) and (g)

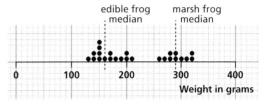

    (c)  10
    (d)  2920 ÷ 10 = 292 grams
    (e)  Median of 290 g marked on dot plot
    (f)  2490 ÷ 15 = 166 grams
    (g)  Median of 160 g marked on dot plot
    (h)  The pupil's answer

**2** (a)  169.5 cm
    (b)  5096 ÷ 30 = 169.9 cm (to 1 d.p.)
    (c)  173 cm
    (d)  The pupil's explanation, for
        example, only $\frac{1}{10}$ of the pupils are
        above the modal height

**3** (a)  63 ÷ 49 = 1.29 bottles per home
    (b)  0
    (c)  1
    (d)  63 ÷ 26 = 2.42 bottles

**4** The pupil's set of numbers, for example
    0, 1, 9, 10, 10

**5** The pupil's set of numbers, for example
    0, 1, 4, 10, 10

# 22 Negative numbers

**Practice booklet** pages 76 to 78

## A **High and deep** (p 167)

This section is to remind pupils of earlier work with negative numbers. You can use the schematic picture to ask difference questions.

## B **Hot and cold** (p 168)

## C **Adding negative numbers** (p 169)

*'The best joke we had was: "Why was Cinderella never chosen for the football team?" … "Because she had a pumpkin for a coach!"'*

◊ It is important to make the distinction between ⁻3 (a quantity which in itself is negative, such as a temperature or a negative score) and – 3 (which means subtract the positive number 3).

◊ When trialling this unit, several teachers held joke contests, with pupils as judges awarding points from ⁻10 to 10. Teachers who did this found their pupils then understood adding and subtracting directed numbers better. If you need to tell some jokes to set the ball rolling, here are some suggestions (of suitably varied quality):

Q: What do you call a camel with three humps?
A: Humphrey

Q: What did the policeman say to his tummy?
A: You're under a vest.

Q: What did the Spanish farmer say to his chickens?
A: Ole!

Focus first on the fact that when you add a set of numbers together any negative number in the set pulls the score down. Check that pupils realise that, for example, ⁻3 + 5 is equal to 5 + ⁻3.

These are the totals for the pictures on the lower half of page 169:
(a) 2   (b) ⁻8   (c) ⁻2   (d) ⁻2   (e) 1   (f) ⁻3

◊ It may be tempting to treat (for example) 5 + ⁻1 as 5 – 1. They give the same answer but they are different things: the first is a preparation for substituting (say) $a = 5$ and $b = ⁻1$ into the formula $p = a + b$; the second is not.

C5, C6  If pupils have not met magic squares before, you may need to demonstrate with one, for example, that has the numbers 1 to 9 in it; its magic number will be 15.

## D Subtracting negative numbers (p 171)

**T**

◊ Again, the idea of taking off a negative score is best understood if it is acted out by pupils. You can tell some story about judges being discovered taking bribes to justify the removal of their scores.

### Ⓐ High and deep (p 167)

**A1** 1191 metres

**A2** (a) Antarctica
    (b) 5637 metres
    (c) The pupil's questions

### Ⓑ Hot and cold (p 168)

**B1** ⁻10°C

**B2** ⁻5°C

**B3** 29 degrees

**B4** 126 degrees

**B5** (a) ⁻5°C
    (b) 1000 m above sea level
    (c) 1700 m
    (d) 700 m

**B6** (a) ⁻2.1°C   (b) ⁻1.7°C   (c) ⁻0.4°C

**B7** ⁻2.3°C, ⁻1.4°C, ⁻1.3°C, ⁻0.7°C, 0.3°C

**B8** 8.2 Celsius degrees

**B9** 5.5 Celsius degrees

**B10** ⁻0.3°C

### Ⓒ Adding negative numbers (p 169)

**C1** (a) ⁻1  (b) ⁻11  (c) 0   (d) ⁻1

**C2** (a) 3     (b) 1     (c) 6
    (d) ⁻4    (e) ⁻3   (f) ⁻3
    (g) 6     (h) 9    (i) 3

**C3** 3°C

**C4** ⁻3°C

**C5** (a)

| 4 | ⁻1 | 0 |
|---|---|---|
| ⁻3 | 1 | 5 |
| 2 | 3 | ⁻2 |

(b)

| 1 | 6 | ⁻1 |
|---|---|---|
| 0 | 2 | 4 |
| 5 | ⁻2 | 3 |

(c)

| ⁻2 | 3 | ⁻4 |
|---|---|---|
| ⁻3 | ⁻1 | 1 |
| 2 | ⁻5 | 0 |

**C6** The pupil's magic square (there are many possibilities)

### Ⓓ Subtracting negative numbers (p 171)

**D1** $1 - {}^-5 = 6$

**D2** $3 - {}^-4 = 7$

**D3** (a) 2     (b) 4     (c) $2 - {}^-2 = 4$

**D4** (a) ⁻9    (b) ⁻1    (c) $^-9 - {}^-8 = {}^-1$

**D5** Make the number positive then add it.

**D6** (a) 12    (b) 22    (c) 32
    (d) 60    (e) 40

**D7** (a) 6     (b) ⁻6    (c) ⁻2
    (d) 25    (e) ⁻17

**D8** (a) 6     (b) ⁻16   (c) 20
    (d) 269   (e) 70    (f) 833

**D9** (a) ⁻13  (b) 20   (c) 9   (d) 89

**D10** $^-10 - {}^-8 = {}^-2$

**D11** (a) $110 - {}^-155$   (b) 265 degrees

### What progress have you made? (p 172)

**1** ⁻2.5, ⁻1.2, ⁻0.9, ⁻0.7, 0.4

**2** (a) 0  (b) ⁻11  (c) 1   (d) ⁻229

**3** (a) 20       (b) 71

**4** (a) ⁻23    (b) 18

**Practice booklet**

## Section A (p 76)

1  150 m

2  3441 m

3  36.2 m

## Section B (p 76)

1  5°C

2  (a)  2°C      (b)  ⁻2°C
   (c)  ⁻1°C     (d)  ⁻20°C

3  It increased by 27 Celsius degrees.

4  There are many possibilities, for example:
   A temperature of 3°C is 9 degrees higher than a temperature of ⁻6°C.
   A temperature of ⁻9°C is 6 degrees lower than a temperature of ⁻3 °C.

5  ⁻1.4°C, ⁻0.9°C, ⁻0.2°C, ⁻0.05°C, ⁻0.01°C, 0.002°C, 0.1°C

## Section C (p 77)

1  (a)  ⁻1      (b)  0      (c)  ⁻4
   (d)  ⁻6      (e)  7      (f)  3

2  ⁻2°C

3  (a)

| -3 | 2 | -5 |
|---|---|---|
| -4 | -2 | 0 |
| 1 | -6 | -1 |

(b)

| 0 | 5 | -2 |
|---|---|---|
| -1 | 1 | 3 |
| 4 | -3 | 2 |

(c)

| 3 | -2 | -1 |
|---|---|---|
| -4 | 0 | 4 |
| 1 | 2 | -3 |

## Section D (p 78)

1  (a)  0       (b)  ⁻6      (c)  ⁻12
   (d)  ⁻2      (e)  1       (f)  ⁻2

2  13

3  (a)  14    (b)  19    (c)  67    (d)  296

4  (a)  7     (b)  8     (c)  ⁻42   (d)  ⁻2

5  (a)  10    (b)  0     (c)  246   (d)  7

6  (a)  166   (b)  19    (c)  21    (d)  ⁻15

# ㉓ Transformations

| Essential | Optional |
|---|---|
| Sheets 172 and 173 | OHP |
| Tracing paper | Transparency of sheet 172 |
| Squared paper | Small mirrors |
| **Practice booklet** pages 79 and 80 | |

## A Reflection (p 173)

> Sheet 172, tracing paper, squared paper
> Optional: Transparency of sheet 172, small mirrors

◊ Pupils can experiment with the picture of Dinah, its images and mirror lines on the top part of sheet 172, using tracing paper or mirrors to check the reflections where necessary. You can lead this work using a transparency of this sheet. If pupils use tracing paper, it is a good idea if they first put an arrow head on the mirror line they are using and trace it when they trace the shape: then the tracing paper can be put in the correct position when it is turned over. An aim of the work is for pupils gradually to reduce their dependence on tracing paper or a mirror, though of course these aids are always useful for checking.

Here and in the later sections, use – and encourage the use of – language like 'the original shape', 'the image after a reflection' and so on.

Negative coordinates are gradually introduced in this section and the next. You may need to do extra practice on plotting and identifying points with negative coordinates.

## B Rotation (p 175)

> Sheets 172 and 173
> Tracing paper, squared paper

Pupils can work on the lower part of sheet 172, which reproduces the quadrilateral, and you can also use a transparency of this sheet to lead the work. Some of these questions may arise as you do so:
  • How do I know when I've completed a half turn?
  • How many degrees are there in a half turn?
  • How many in a quarter turn?
The importance of giving a full description of a rotation (centre, angle, direction) should be stressed.

◊ The rotations in B2(c) (on sheet 173) are quite challenging, as the position of each centre of rotation is not obvious.

## ℂ **Translation** (p 173)

| Squared paper |
| --- |

◊ Karl's error in C2 shows the need to concentrate on what happens to a particular point on the starting shape (in this case the bottom right-hand corner of the triangle) when a translation occurs.

◊ Column vector notation is not used at this stage but you could introduce it now if you wish.

◊ In introducing the 'Patterns with transformations' activity to pupils, you may need to stress that they should describe what needs to be done to the *original design* to get each part of the pattern, not what needs to be done to the part of the pattern they have just dealt with.

## 𝔸 **Reflection** (p 173)

**A1**

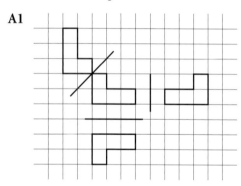

**A2** (a) V  (b) X  (c) W  (d) U

**A3** (a) E  (b) C  (c) G  (d) J

**A4** (a) M4  (b) M5  (c) M1  (d) M1

**A5**

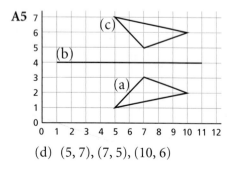

(d) (5, 7), (7, 5), (10, 6)

**A6**

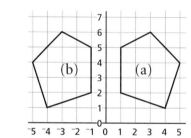

(c) (⁻1, 2), (⁻4, 1), (⁻5, 4), (⁻3, 6), (⁻1, 5)
In each pair of coordinates the first (across) number has become negative.

## 𝔹 **Rotation** (p 175)

**B1**

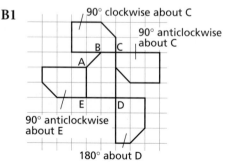

**B2** The pupil's rotations on sheet 173

124 • *23 Transformations*

**B3** (a) W      (b) X      (c) Z

      (d) Y      (e) U

**B4** (a) Centre A, 180°

      (b) Centre C, 90° clockwise

      (c) Centre B, 180°

      (d) Centre B, 180°

**B5** (a), (b)

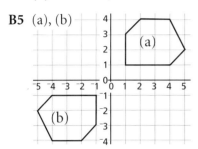

      (c) (⁻1, ⁻1), (⁻1, ⁻3), (⁻2, ⁻4), (⁻4, ⁻4),
         (⁻5, ⁻2), (⁻4, ⁻1)
        All the coordinates (up and across)
        have become negative.

## Transformation code

The two words are STONE and NOSE.

For TASTE, starting at T:
      Reflect in M4
      Reflect in M2
      Rotate a half turn, centre C
      Reflect in M2

For ROTATE, starting at R:
      Rotate a half turn, centre C
      Rotate a quarter turn clockwise, centre C
      Reflect in M4
      Reflect in M4
      Reflect in M2

### ℂ Translation (p 178)

**C1** (a) E    (b) B    (c) C    (d) G

**C2** He is not correct; the translation is 4
      units right, 1 unit up.

**C3** (a) 2 units right, 1 unit up

      (b) 2 units left, 1 unit up

      (c) 4 units left, 2 units down

      (d) 4 units right, 2 units down

**C4** (a)

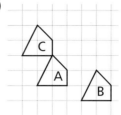

      (b) 4 units left, 3 units up

      (c) 4 units right, 3 units down

## Patterns with transformations

**1** (a) Reflect design in line M4

      (b) Rotate design 180° about O

      (c) Reflect design in M2

**2** (a) Rotate design 90° clockwise about O

      (b) Rotate design 180° about O

      (c) Rotate design 90° anticlockwise
         about O

**3** (a) Rotate design 90° clockwise about O

      (b) Reflect design in M1

      (c) Reflect design in M2

### What progress have you made? (p 179)

**1**

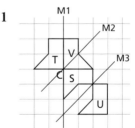

**2** (a) A translation 3 units right, 3 down

      (b) A reflection in M1

## Sections A, B and C (p 79)

**1**

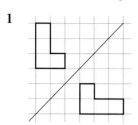

**2**

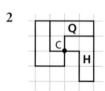

**3**

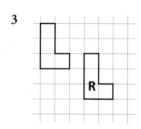

**4**

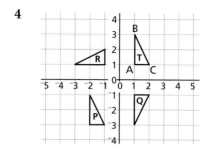

| | A | B | C |
|---|---|---|---|
| T, the original triangle | (1, 1) | (1, 3) | (2, |
| P, a translation of T, 3 units left, 4 units down | (⁻2, ⁻3) | (⁻2, ⁻1) | (⁻1, |
| Q, a reflection of T in the horizontal axis | (1, ⁻1) | (1, ⁻3) | (2, ⁻ |
| R, a rotation of T, 90° anticlockwise about (0, 0) | (⁻1, 1) | (⁻3, 1) | (⁻1, |

For P, the first coordinate in each pair has become 3 units smaller and the second coordinate has become 4 units smaller.

For Q, the first coordinate in each pair has stayed the same, while the second coordinate has become negative.

For R, the coordinates have swapped over and the new first coordinate has become negative.

**5** 1 unit left, 2 units down

# ㉔ Functions and graphs

| Essential | Optional |
|---|---|
| 2 mm graph paper | OHP |
| Squared paper | |

**Practice booklet** pages 81 and 82 (graph paper needed)

## Ⓐ **From table to graph** (p 180)

> 2 mm graph paper

◊ The main points to be covered in the introduction are:
  • We can make a table from a rule given in words.
  • The values in the table can be plotted as points.
  • When the variables are continuous, a line can be drawn through the points to show the relationship between the variables.

You should point out that real-life situations rarely give precise straight-line graphs (except in cases where linearity is built in, as for example with currency conversion graphs).

## Ⓑ **Using formulas** (p 182)

**B5** For the first time in this unit the pupil has to find a rule from some number pairs.

## Ⓒ **Functions** (p 184)

> Optional: OHP

The activity referred to on page 185 is similar to 'Spot the rule' in *Book 1*. You will need a large grid on the board or OHP with $x$ and $y$ axes.

◊ You can start the activity by telling the class that you are thinking of a rule linking $x$ and $y$, for example $y = x + 2$. Ask a member of the class to give you a value of $x$; work out $y$ and plot the corresponding point on the grid. Continue until someone can tell you your rule.

Then ask a pupil to take over with a rule of their own.

◊ If pupils are adventurous and use rules involving, for example, squaring, then you can ask what kinds of rule give points which lie in a straight line.

◊ If nobody else does so, use a rule like $x + y = 6$.

◊ Ask pupils if they see any similarities and differences between earlier work on sequences and this work. They should be able to appreciate that

- in the case of a sequence, $n$ is restricted to being a whole number (discrete), whereas $x$ is continuous
- the values of $y$ for $x = 1, 2, 3, 4, \ldots$ form a sequence (which helps when pupils are trying to find the equation of a linear graph).

## Ⓓ Negative numbers on graphs (p 186)

| Squared paper |
|---|

◊ This work shows that calculations involving negative numbers continue a straight line in the expected way.

## Ⓐ From table to graph (p 180)

A1 (a)

| Gas in tank (kg) | Hours away from base |
|---|---|
| 1 | 1 |
| 2 | 3 |
| 3 | 5 |
| 4 | 7 |
| 5 | 9 |
| 6 | 11 |
| 7 | 13 |

(b) The pupil's graph of points from the table, joined with a straight line

(c) 8 hours　　(d) $5\frac{1}{2}$ kg

A2 (a)

| $t$ | 0 | 1 | 2 | 3 | 4 | 5 | 6 |
|---|---|---|---|---|---|---|---|
| $h$ | 20 | 50 | 80 | 110 | 140 | 170 | 200 |

(b) The pupil's graph of points from the table

(c) 65 cm

(d) $\frac{1}{2}$ hour

(e) 2 hours 40 minutes

(f) 95

A3 (a)

| $t$ | 0 | 1 | 2 | 3 | 4 | 5 | 6 |
|---|---|---|---|---|---|---|---|
| $l$ | 28 | 26 | 24 | 22 | 20 | 18 | 16 |

(b) The pupil's graph of points from the table

(c) 21 cm　　(d) $5\frac{1}{2}$ hours

(e) $1\frac{1}{2}$　　(f) 19

## Ⓑ Using formulas (p 182)

B1 (a) $c = 4d + 2$　　(b) $c = 3d + 3$

(c) $c = 5d$

B2 (a) £11　　(b) £23　　(c) £51

(d) £71　　(e) £13

B3 (a)

| $d$ | 1 | 2 | 3 | 4 | 5 | 6 | 7 |
|---|---|---|---|---|---|---|---|
| $c$ | 6 | 11 | 16 | 21 | 26 | 31 | 36 |

(b) The pupil's graph of points from the table, labelled $c = 5d + 1$

(c) £28.50

(d) $3\frac{1}{2}$ miles

B4 (a)

(b) (i) 5 miles (ii) $3\frac{1}{2}$ miles

(iii) $4\frac{1}{4}$ miles

(c) Nothing!

(d) Applying the rule strictly you would pay ⁻£1, meaning perhaps that the taxi firm would pay you £1; but this is not very likely!

**B5** (a)

| Weight on spring, $w$ kg | 0 | 1 | 2 | 3 | 4 | 5 |
|---|---|---|---|---|---|---|
| Length of spring, $l$ cm | **15** | **25** | **35** | **45** | **55** | **65** |

(b) $l = 10w + 15$

(c)

| Weight on spring, $w$ kg | 0 | 1 | 2 | 3 | 4 | 5 |
|---|---|---|---|---|---|---|
| Length of spring, $w$ cm | 20 | 25 | 30 | 35 | 40 | 45 |

(d) $l = 5w + 20$

ℂ **Functions** (p 184)

**C1** (a)

| $x$ | 0 | 1 | 2 | 3 | 4 | 5 | 6 |
|---|---|---|---|---|---|---|---|
| $y$ | 1 | **2** | **3** | **4** | **5** | **6** | **7** |

(b)

| $x$ | 1 | 2 | 3 | 4 |
|---|---|---|---|---|
| $y$ | **1** | **3** | **5** | **7** |

(c)

| $x$ | 0 | 1 | 2 | 3 | 4 | 5 |
|---|---|---|---|---|---|---|
| $y$ | 5 | **4** | **3** | **2** | **1** | **0** |

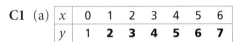

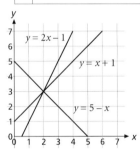

**C2**

**C3**

| $x$ | 0 | 1 | 2 | 3 |
|---|---|---|---|---|
| $y$ | 4 | 7 | **10** | **13** |

$y = 3x + 4$

**C4**

| $x$ | 0 | 1 | 2 | 3 | 4 |
|---|---|---|---|---|---|
| $y$ | 10 | **9** | **8** | **7** | **6** |

This was Ted's rule.

**C5** $y = 2x + 1$

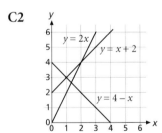

**C6** $y = x + 3$

**C7** Owen

**C8** Trevor

𝔻 **Negative numbers from graphs**
(p 186)

**D1** (a)

| $x$ | 0 | 1 | 2 | 3 | 4 | 5 |
|---|---|---|---|---|---|---|
| $y$ | ⁻7 | ⁻**5** | ⁻**3** | ⁻**1** | **1** | **3** |

(b) The pupil's graph of points from the table

(c) 2

(d) $2\frac{1}{2}$

**D2** (a)

| $x$ | 0 | 1 | 2 | 3 | 4 | 5 |
|---|---|---|---|---|---|---|
| $y$ | ⁻**3** | ⁻**2** | ⁻**1** | **0** | **1** | **2** |

(b) The pupil's graph of points from the table

**D3** (a)

| $x$ | ⁻3 | ⁻2 | ⁻1 | 0 | 1 | 2 | 3 |
|---|---|---|---|---|---|---|---|
| $y$ | ⁻2 | ⁻**1** | **0** | **1** | **2** | **3** | **4** |

(b) The pupil's graph of points from the table

**D4** (a)

| $x$ | ⁻3 | ⁻2 | ⁻1 | 0 | 1 | 2 | 3 |
|---|---|---|---|---|---|---|---|
| $y$ | ⁻**4** | ⁻**3** | ⁻**2** | ⁻**1** | **0** | **1** | **2** |

(b) The pupil's graph of points from the table

**What progress have you made?** (p 187)

**1** (a)

| $t$ | 0 | 1 | 2 | 3 | 4 | 5 |
|---|---|---|---|---|---|---|
| $c$ | **10** | **25** | **40** | **55** | **70** | **85** |

(b) The pupil's graph of points from the table

**2** $3\frac{1}{2}$ hours

**3**

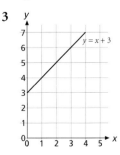

**4**

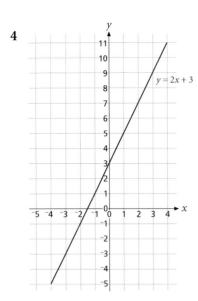

$y = 2x + 3$

**5** (a) $y = 2x + 2$   (b) $y = 7 - x$

## Practice booklet

## Sections A and B (p 81)

**1** (a)

| $t$ | 0 | 1 | 2 | 3 | 4 | 5 |
|---|---|---|---|---|---|---|
| $d$ | 80 | 100 | **120** | **140** | **160** | **180** |

(b) $d = 80 + 20t$

(c) The pupil's graph of points from the table

(d) $t = 2.4$

**2** (a)

| $t$ | 0 | 1 | 2 | 3 | 4 | 5 |
|---|---|---|---|---|---|---|
| $d$ | 30 | **26** | **22** | **18** | **14** | **10** |

(b) The pupil's graph of points from the table

(c) 3.5 minutes

## Sections C and D (p 82)

**1** (a)

| $x$ | 0 | 1 | 2 | 3 | 4 | 5 | 6 | 7 | 8 |
|---|---|---|---|---|---|---|---|---|---|
| $y$ | 8 | 7 | 6 | 5 | 4 | 3 | 2 | 1 | 0 |

(b) The pupil's labelled graph of $y = 8 - x$

**2** (a)

| $x$ | ⁻4 | ⁻3 | ⁻2 | ⁻1 | 0 | 1 | 2 | 3 | 4 |
|---|---|---|---|---|---|---|---|---|---|
| $y$ | ⁻12 | ⁻10 | ⁻8 | ⁻6 | ⁻4 | ⁻2 | 0 | 2 | 4 |

(b) The pupil's labelled graph of $y = 2x - 4$

**3** (a) $y = 3x + 2$
   (b) $y = 7$
   (c) $y = x - 2$
   (d) $y = 6 - x$

**4** $h = 35 - 5w$

**Multiples and factors**

<table>
<tr><td>Essential</td><td>Optional</td></tr>
<tr><td>Sheets 134 and 174 to 176<br>Dice, counters (two colours)<br>Sheet 177 (or other polygon tiles)<br><br>Practice booklet pages 83 to 86</td><td>OHP transparency of sheet 175</td></tr>
</table>

## A **Multiples** (p 188)

### Nasty multiples

*'This game is very good. I enjoyed playing it and the pupils sometimes beat me.'*

> Each pair needs sheet 174, a dice and several counters of two colours

After revising the idea of a multiple, pupils can consolidate their knowledge by playing the game.

## B **Factors** (p 189)

> Sheets 175 and 134 (for the sieve of Eratosthenes)
> Optional: OHP transparency of sheet 175

The factor chart makes it possible to see and discuss patterns.

◊ You could get the class to make a large factor chart on squared paper for numbers up to, say, 80. Groups could be given different ranges of numbers to work on.

One teacher tried this and reported:

'I split the class to work in fours, one pair to do factors of 1–45, the other 40–80. I was then going to overlap them for display. Students found the activity difficult, some didn't immediately see the patterns. 40–80 was a disaster area! For 1–45, about half the pairs managed successfully. BUT ... the quality of discussion and language and understanding the activity generated was EXCELLENT, the work for display not very good!'

◊ A popular game (not referred to in the pupil's book) is 'Factor bingo'.

Ask each pupil to write down seven numbers which are to be factors. They can repeat (for example, 2, 2, 3, 3, 4, 6, 7). They are not allowed to use 1, but if they suggest it, reward their perspicacity!

Make a list of 'multiples' for yourself and read them out one at a time. Include the occasional prime number!

Pupils can cross out any factor of the number you read out. They are not allowed to cross out a number more than once. For example, if a pupil's list includes 2, 2, 4, 8 and the number read out is 16, they can cross out one of the 2s, the 4 and the 8.

For the first couple of games you can check after each number what factors could have been crossed off.

## C Multiples and factors (p 190)

> Sheet 176 (for the 'Multiples and factors maze')

## D Divisibility (p 191)

> Sheet 134 (for question D5)

## E Common multiples (p 192)

## F Common factors (p 193)

## G Common factors and multiples (p 194)

## H Polygon wheels (p 195)

> Polygon tiles, from sheet 177 or elsewhere (for example ATM polygon mats); an OHP is very useful.

◊ If you demonstrate with polygons on the OHP, cut a small slit in an edge to represent the dot.

After a couple of turns of the square about the pentagon, you could ask:
  • Will the dots ever come together again?
  • If so, how many turns do you think it will take, and why?

◊ Pupils may jump to the conclusion that the number of turns is found by multiplying the numbers of sides of the two polygons. If so, you can ask them to find out if this is always true.

The number of turns is the lowest common multiple of both numbers of sides. For example, for a square rolling round a hexagon the number of turns is the lowest common multiple of 4 and 6, that is 12.

## ⒜ Multiples (p 188)

**A1** 3, 9, 12, 30, 33

**A2** 8, 16, 24, 48, 56

**A3** (a) Any five multiples of 10
(b) 70, 90, 100, 110, 170, 220
(c) The last digit is 0.

**A4** (a) 6, 8, 18, 20, 24, 36, 60
(b) 6, 15, 18, 24, 36, 60
(c) 8, 20, 24, 36, 60
(d) 15, 20, 60

**A5** 33p, 59p , 66p

**A6** (a) 12 is a multiple of 1, 2, 3, 4, 6 and 12.
(b) 15 is a multiple of 1, 3, 5 and 15.
(c) 24 is a multiple of 1, 2, 3, 4, 6, 8, 12 and 24.
(d) 30 is a multiple of 1, 2, 3, 5, 6, 10, 15 and 30.

## ⒝ Factors (p 189)

**B1** (a) 1 2 3 4 6 12
(b) 1 2 3 6 9 18
(c) 1 2 3 4 6 8 12 24
(d) 1 2 3 5 6 10 15 30

**B2** (a) 1 2 3 4 6 9 12 18 36
One factor pairs off with itself.
(b) 36 has an **odd** number of factors.
(c) Any three square numbers
(d) They are square numbers, with one factor pairing off with itself.

**B3** 1 7
There are only two factors, 1 and the number itself.

**B4** 2, 3, 5, 7, 11, 13

**B5** 23 and 29

**B6** Possible numbers are 13, 17, 37 and so on.

## ⒞ Multiples and factors (p 190)

**C1** (a) 6 is a **multiple** of 2.
(b) 6 is a **factor** of 30.
(c) 10 is a **factor** of 60.
(d) 8 is a **factor** of 32.
(e) 8 is a **multiple** of 4.
(f) 36 is a **multiple** of 9.

**C2** (a) 1, 5, 25
(b) 25, 50, 75, 100, 150

**C3** 40, 80, 120

**C4** 1, 2, 3, 4, 5, 6, 10, 12, 60

**C5** (a) The pupil's four multiples of 6
(b) 1, 2, 3, 6

**Multiples and factors maze**

## ⒟ Divisibility (p 191)

**D1** (a) 562, 3334, 3108, 874, 678, 400 098, 67 924
(b) If the last digit is 0, 2, 4, 6 or 8, the number is divisible by 2.
(c) The last digit is 6, so the number is divisible by 2.

**D2** (a) If the last digit is 0, then the number is divisible by 10.
(b) If the last digit is 0 or 5, then the number is divisible by 5.
(c) (i) 2390, 60, 1200, 7810
(ii) 2390, 765, 7415, 60, 7810, 1200

**D3** (a) $782\,654 \div 3 = 260\,884.666\,66\ldots$
The decimal part tells us that
$782\,654$ is not divisible by 3.

(b) (i)

| 4056 | Yes | 15 | Yes |
|------|-----|----|-----|
| 1101 | **Yes** | **3** | **Yes** |
| 692 | No | 17 | No |
| 9218 | **No** | **20** | **No** |

(ii) The pupil's numbers
in the table

(c) If the sum of the digits is divisible by
3, then the number is divisible by 3.

(d) 3108, 678, 4893, 400 098

**D4** (a) The pupil's numbers that are
divisible by 9 and their digit sums

(b) The pupil's numbers that are not
divisible by 9 and their digit sums

(c) If the digit sum is divisible by 9, then
the number is divisible by 9.

(d) 504, 21 348, 39 285, 61 236

**D5** (a) The pupil's hundred square with
each multiple of 2 underlined

(b) The pupil's hundred square with a
circle round each multiple of 3

(c) Numbers divisible by 6 are divisible
by 2 and 3.

(d) (i) 106, 138, 1314, 5012, 135 912
(ii) 138, 1314, 213, 135 912
(iii) 138, 1314, 135 912

*****D6** (a) If the last two digits are divisible by
4, then the number is divisible by 4.

(b) If the last three digits are divisible by
8, then the number is divisible by 8.

**E  Common multiples** (p 192)

**E1** (a) Multiples of 3: 3, 6, 9, 12, 15, 18,
21, 24, 27, 30
Multiples of 5: 5, 10, 15, 20, 25,
30, 35, 40, 45, 50

(b) Three common multiples of 3 and 5
such as 15, 30 and 45

(c) 15

**E2** (a) 4, 8, 12, 16, 20, 24, 28, 32, 36, 40

(b) 6, 12, 18, 24, 30, 36, 42, 48, 54, 60

(c) Three common multiples of 4 and 6
such as 12, 24 and 36

(d) 12

**E3** (a) Four common multiples of 2 and 5
such as 10, 20, 30 and 40

(b) 10

**E4** (a) 6      (b) 18      (c) 6

**E5** (a) 30      (b) 12      (c) 6

**F  Common factors** (p 193)

**F1** (a) 1, 3, 5, 15      (b) 1, 2, 4, 5, 10, 20

(c) 1 and 5      (d) 5

**F2** (a) 1, 2, 3 and 6   (b) 6

**F3** 2

**F4** (a) 3      (b) 8      (c) 1

**F5** 4

**G  Common factors and multiples** (p 194)

**G1** (a) 20      (b) 2

**G2** (a) 24      (b) 1

**G3** 20 seconds

**G4** 4p

**G5** 30 sweets

**G6** 6 cm by 6 cm square tiles

**G7**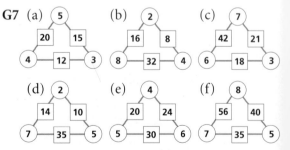

**What progress have you made?** (p 195)

**1** The pupil's three multiples of 5

**2** Three factors of 24 from 1, 2, 3, 4, 6, 8,
12 and 24

**3** 2, 3, 5, 7, 11, 13, 17 and 19

**4** The last digit (6) tells you that the number is even and so it cannot be prime.

**5** 21        **6** 12

## Practice booklet

### Sections A, B and C (p 83)

**1** (a) 6, 8, 10, 30, 90, 100, 110
(b) 10, 30, 75, 90, 100, 110
(c) 6, 30, 90    (d) 10, 30, 90, 100, 110

**2** (a) 1, 2, 4, 8     (b) 1, 3, 9
(c) 1, 3, 5, 15     (d) 1, 2, 4, 5, 10, 20
(e) 1, 3           (f) 1, 2, 4
(g) 1, 7           (h) 1, 13

**3** 33, 63

**4** (a) 5 is a **factor** of 10.
(b) 20 is a **multiple** of 4.
(c) 18 is a **multiple** of 6.
(d) 18 is a **multiple** of 3.
(e) 9 is a **factor** of 18.
(f) 60 is a **multiple** of 10.
(g) 3 is a **factor** of 6.
(h) 6 is a **factor** of 24.
(i) 24 is a **multiple** of 8.

**5** 1 2 **4** 5 **10** 20 25 **50 100**

**6** 6, 36

**7** 1, 2, 3, 6, 7, 14, 21, 42

**8** 2, 11, 19, 23, 29

### Section D (p 84)

**1** (a) 340, 156, 120, 7000, 902, 650, 4008
(b) 340, 265, 6755, 120, 7000, 3265, 650
(c) 340, 120, 7000, 650

**2** (a)

| Number | Digit sum |
|--------|-----------|
| 471 | 12 |
| 1260 | 9 |
| 856 | 19 |
| 4734 | 18 |
| 1382 | 14 |
| 5853 | 21 |
| 109 832 | 23 |

(b) 471, 1260, 4734, 5853
(c) 1260, 4734

**3** (a) 402, 347 622, 57 674
(b) 402, 347 622, 5013, 9831
(c) 402, 347 622

**4** 561

**5** 487

**\*6** (a) 7924, 1504, 2840, 35 112
(b) 1504, 2840, 35 112

### Sections E, F and G (p 85)

**1** (a) 4, 8, 12, 16, 20, 24, 28, 32, 36, 40
(b) 3, 6, 9, 12, 15, 18, 21, 24, 27, 30
(c) Any three common multiples of 4 and 3 such as 12, 24 and 36
(d) 12

**2** (a) Any four common multiples of 2 and 6 such as 6, 12, 18 and 24
(b) 6

**3** (a) 30      (b) 14      (c) 8

**4** (a) 1, 2, 7, 14    (b) 1, 5, 7, 35
(c) 1, 7           (d) 7

**5** (a) 1, 2, 4      (b) 4

**6** (a) 5        (b) 4        (c) 1

**7** 40 seconds

**8** All possible prices are 1p, 2p, 3p, 4p, 5p, 6p, 10p, 12p, 15p, 20p, 30p and 60p

**9** 28 is the smallest possible number of pupils. As 56 (the next possible number) is rather large for a class, the number of pupils is probably 28.

**10** (a)    (b)    (c)

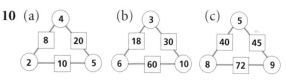

# Know your calculator

---

**Essential**

Scientific calculators
Sheets 179 to 181 (for the game 'Operation 3062')

**Practice booklet** pages 87 to 92

---

## 𝔸 **In order** (p 196)

Pupils investigate the rules used by a scientific calculator to evaluate expressions that use two operations to arrive at the priority rules for dealing with multiplication, division, addition and subtraction.

The game 'Operation 3062' consolidates the use of these rules.

Scientific calculators (one for each pupil)

◊ You could begin by asking pupils to predict what they think their calculators will give for each set of key presses on page 196. Pupils find the result of each set of key presses (remind them they need to press the '=' key or 'ENTER' key at the end) and try to describe the rules they think the calculator uses to evaluate expressions that use any combination of the four operations. They should try their rules out on their own expressions. Working in groups, each group could try to produce a clear statement of the rules they think the calculator uses.

A brief statement of the rules could be

- You multiply or divide before you add or subtract.
- Otherwise, work from left to right.

Once pupils understand these rules, point out that they are widely used in numerical calculations and they should use them for the rest of the unit.

◊ Some calculators use the symbols * and / for × and ÷ respectively. Pupils with these calculators need to interpret the × key press as * and the ÷ key press as /.

**A6**  Pupils could consider how many different results are possible. They could make up their own puzzles like this for someone else to solve.

## A7 Operation 3062

This game consolidates the priority rules for multiplication, division, addition and subtraction.

> Sheet 179 (one copy of the rules and board for each group)
> Sheet 180 (two sheets on card for each group)
> Sheet 181 (one sheet on card for each group)

◊ Calculators should not be used for the game.

◊ Sheets 180 and 181 need to be copied on to card so that the operations and numbers do not show through.

◊ Here is full set of results for 'Operation 3062':

| | | | |
|---|---|---|---|
| $30 + 6 + 2 = 38$ | $30 - 6 + 2 = 26$ | $30 \times 6 + 2 = 182$ | $30 \div 6 + 2 = 7$ |
| $30 + 6 - 2 = 34$ | $30 - 6 - 2 = 22$ | $30 \times 6 - 2 = 178$ | $30 \div 6 - 2 = 3$ |
| $30 + 6 \times 2 = 42$ | $30 - 6 \times 2 = 18$ | $30 \times 6 \times 2 = 360$ | $30 \div 6 \times 2 = 10$ |
| $30 + 6 \div 2 = 33$ | $30 - 6 \div 2 = 27$ | $30 \times 6 \div 2 = 90$ | $30 \div 6 \div 2 = 2.5$ |

◊ You may wish to adapt the board and result cards so that pupils can play the game with a different set of numbers (that could lead to negative results).

One suggestion is:  | 16 |   | 8 |   | 4 | = |

with result cards:

| 28 | 20 | 48 | 18 | 4 | 12 |
|---|---|---|---|---|---|
| ⁻16 | 14 | 512 | 132 | 124 | 32 |
| 0.5 | 8 | 6 | ⁻2 | | |

◊ Pupils could design game boards and result cards for other groups to use.

## B  Brackets (p 197)

> Pupils do the questions without a calculator but could use a calculator to check their results.

## C  A thin dividing line (p 198)

> Some calculators use a line to show division. Pupils with calculators like this should not use them for C1 and C2.

## D  All keyed up (p 199)

> ◊  Not all brackets keys are the same. For example on some calculators the brackets keys look like this:  $[(---$    $---)]$
>
> Make sure pupils know which keys to use on their calculators.

**D5**  Pupils could write an appropriate expression for each set of key presses.

> ◊  Pupils could use a spreadsheet to investigate the value of the expression $a \lozenge b \lozenge c$ for various values of $a$, $b$ and $c$ where each diamond can be replaced by any one of the four operations and brackets can be used. The spreadsheet could be set up as shown below.

|    | A | B | C |
|----|---|---|---|
| 1  | 10 | | |
| 2  | 5 | | |
| 3  | 2 | | |
| 4  | | | |
| 5  | =A1+A2+A3 | =(A1+A2)+A3 | =A1+(A2+A3) |
| 6  | =A1+A2−A3 | =(A1+A2)−A3 | =A1+(A2−A3) |
| 7  | =A1+A2*A3 | =(A1+A2)*A3 | =A1+(A2*A3) |
| 8  | =A1+A2/A3 | =(A1+A2)/A3 | =A1+(A2/A3) |
| 9  | | | |
| 10 | =A1−A2+A3 | =(A1−A2)+A3 | =A1−(A2+A3 |
| 11 | =A1−A2−A3 | =(A1−A2)−A3 | =A1−(A2−A |
| 12 | =A1−A2*A3 | =(A1−A2)*A3 | 1−(A2*A |
| 13 | =A1−A2/A3 | =(A1−A2)/A3 | |
| 14 | | | |
| 15 | =A1*A2+A3 | =(A1*A2)+A | |
| 16 | =A1*A2−A3 | = | |
| 17 | =A1*A2 | = | |
| 18 | =A1*A | | |
| 19 | | | |

The investigation will be much easier if pupils have a separate note of the expressions in each cell possibly in the form below:

|   | A | B | C |
|---|---|---|---|
| 1 | a | | |
| 2 | b | | |
| 3 | c | | |
| 4 | | | |
| 5 | a + b + c | (a + b) + c | a + (b + c) |
| 6 | a + b − c | (a + b) − c | a + (b − c) |
| 7 | a + b × c | (a + b) × c | a + (b × c) |
| 8 | a + b ÷ c | (a + b) ÷ c | a + (b ÷ c) |
| 9 | | | |
| 10 | a − b + c | (a − b) + c | a − (b + c) |
| 11 | a − b − c | (a − b) − c | a − (b − c) |
| 12 | a − b × c | (a − b) × c | (b × c) |
| 13 | a − b ÷ c | (a − b) ÷ c | |
| 14 | | | |
| 15 | a × b + c | (a − b) + | |
| 16 | a × b − c | ( | |
| 17 | a × b | | |
| 18 | a × b | | |
| 19 | | | |

One outcome is confirmation of the priority rules,
for example that $a + b \times c = a + (b \times c)$ for all values of $a$, $b$ and $c$.

Pupils could consider:

- Which values for $a$, $b$ and $c$ give a set of positive results?
- Which values give a set of integer results?
- Which values give a set of non-recurring decimals?
- What happens if $a$, $b$ or $c$ has a value of 1? or 0?
- Which values give 16 different answers in the first column? Which values give repeats and why?
- What happens if two values are equal? What about three equal values?
- Which expressions always have the same value and why?
  For example,     $a − b − c = a − (b + c)$ and
  $$a \div b \div c = a \div (b \times c)$$
- Why do some rows always give three identical results?
  For example,     $a + b + c = (a + b) + c = a + (b + c)$
  $$a \times b \div c = (a \times b) \div c = a \times (b \div c)$$

E **Memory** (p 201)

◊ Some calculators use the same key to store and recall so you may have to discuss the 'shift' or '2nd function' key.

T

E2 Emphasise that pupils can use any method they feel confident with: for example, some may feel much happier using the brackets keys throughout. More confident pupils could think about different ways to carry out each calculation and hence check their results.

## F  Squares (p 201)

Some calculators use the same key for squares and square roots so you may have to discuss the 'shift' or '2nd function' key.

## G  Square roots (p 202)

## H  Negative numbers (p 203)

## I  Complex calculations (p 204)

## A  In order (p 196)

**A1** (a) 5    (b) 7    (c) 7*    (d) 7*
    (e) 0    (f) 6

* Pupils who give 8 and 5 as their answers for (c) and (d) respectively are probably consistently working from left to right.

**A2** A, B, E and F

**A3** The pupil's sets of key presses with result 8

**A4** (a) 4    (b) 7    (c) 10    (d) 2
     (e) 4    (f) 5    (g) 8    (h) 30
     (i) 23    (j) 12    (k) 9    (l) 2
     (m) 20    (n) 5    (o) 13

**A5** (a) 6    (b) 6    (c) 2    (d) 4
     (e) 9    (f) 8    (g) 12    (h) 4
     (i) 5

**A6** (a) $12 + 6 - 2$    (b) $12 \times 6 - 2$
     (c) $12 + 6 \times 2$    (d) $12 + 6 \div 2$

## B  Brackets (p 197)

**B1** (a) 12    (b) 2    (c) 2    (d) 15
     (e) 2    (f) 2    (g) 4    (h) 16
     (i) 3

**B2** (a) 12    (b) 14    (c) 5    (d) 11
     (e) 5    (f) 3    (g) 5    (h) 7

**B3** (a) 3    (b) 6    (c) 3    (d) 11

**B4** A, C and E

## C  A thin dividing line (p 198)

**C1** A and C    B and G    D and F    H and I

**C2** (a) $10 + \frac{6}{2}$      (b) $\frac{18 - 2}{4}$

     (c) $\frac{8 + 4}{3}$      (d) $12 - \frac{10}{5}$

     (e) $\frac{5}{3 - 1}$      (f) $\frac{12}{4} + 2$

**C3** (a) 7    (b) 14    (c) 4    (d) 3
     (e) 2    (f) 12    (g) 10    (h) 2
     (i) 15

## Ⓓ All keyed up (p 199)

**D1** (a) 2     (b) 15     (c) 5

**D2** (a) 5*     (b) 5     (c) 37
     (d) 4     (e) 35     (f) 5

  * Pupils who give 19 as their answer for (a) have probably keyed in $16 + 24 \div 8$ omitting the necessary brackets.

**D3** (a) 9     (b) 13     (c) 9
     (d) 4     (e) 28     (f) 1.6

**D4** (a) (i) 19    (ii) 27    (iii) 9    (iv) 5
     (b) The pupil's description

**D5** (a) 15     (b) 5     (c) 2

**D6** A and C

**D7** $\boxed{9}\ \boxed{-}\ \boxed{3}\ \boxed{=}\ \boxed{\div}\ \boxed{2}$
   or
   $\boxed{(}\ \boxed{9}\ \boxed{-}\ \boxed{3}\ \boxed{)}\ \boxed{\div}\ \boxed{2}$

**D8** (a) 9     (b) 46     (c) 2.5
     (d) 22.1     (e) 3.8     (f) 0.5
     (g) 7     (h) 4     (i) 15

## Ⓔ Memory (p 201)

**E1** (a) 59     (b) 2     (c) 0.25
     (d) 13.5     (e) 8.2     (f) 100

**E2** (a) 1.2     (b) 25.97     (c) 60
     (d) 6.5     (e) 469     (f) 42

**E3** (a) 1.5 gallons    (b) 5.3 gallons
     (c) 2.7 gallons    (d) 39.6 gallons

## Ⓕ Squares (p 201)

**F1** (a) 441     (b) 3969     (c) 11 664
     (d) 96 721     (e) 2500

**F2** (a) 19    (b) 28    (c) 300    (d) 67

**F3** 625

**F4** (a) 2304 ($48^2$)     (b) 2116 ($46^2$)

**F5** (a) 818 m$^2$     (b) 456 m$^2$

**F6** Yes, 17 stones on each side

**F7** No

**F8** (a) 10.24    (b) 32.49    (c) 2.1316
     (d) 0.64    (e) 0.0144

**F9** (a) 1.9   (b) 4.8   (c) 0.9   (d) 1.05

## Ⓖ Square roots (p 202)

**G1** (a) 5     (b) 2     (c) 7
     (d) 10     (e) 1

**G2** (a) 4     (b) 9     (c) 6
     (d) 8     (e) 12

**G3** (a) 11     (b) 15     (c) 20
     (d) 69     (e) 59

**G4** (a) 6.5     (b) 3.7     (c) 1.28
     (d) 0.6     (e) 0.04

**G5** (a) 3000
     (b) The pupil's own estimates; if each person stands in a metre square the board will be 3 km wide.

## Ⓗ Negative numbers (p 203)

**H1** (a) (i) 5    (ii) 4    (iii) ⁻5    (iv) ⁻6
     (b) The pupil's checks

**H2** (a) 1     (b) ⁻5     (c) ⁻8
     (d) ⁻4     (e) ⁻6     (f) ⁻7
     (g) ⁻4     (h) ⁻20

**H3** (a) 10     (b) 8     (c) ⁻3
     (d) 1     (e) ⁻8.5     (f) ⁻8.1
     (g) 4.9     (h) ⁻4.1

**H4** (a) 2     (b) ⁻2     (c) 5
     (d) ⁻7     (e) ⁻5     (f) ⁻5

## Ⓘ Complex calculations (p 204)

**I1** (a) 25   (b) 4   (c) 50   (d) 22
     (e) 3   (f) 25   (g) 35   (h) 35
     (i) 12   (j) 11   (k) 4   (l) 3

**I2** (a) 18   (b) 36   (c) 3   (d) 81

**I3** (a) $\boxed{5}\ \boxed{\times}\ \boxed{7}\ \boxed{x^2}$

(b) $\boxed{5}\ \boxed{+}\ \boxed{7}\ \boxed{x^2}$

(c) $\boxed{1}\ \boxed{0}\ \boxed{0}\ \boxed{\div}\ \boxed{5}\ \boxed{x^2}$

**I4** (a) 12.06    (b) 625    (c) 60.25
(d) 3721    (e) 171.396    (f) 3.56
(g) 7.9    (h) 1.5    (i) 36
(j) 7.44    (k) 30    (l) 9

**I5**

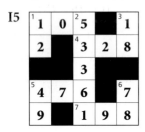

## What progress have you made? (p 205)

1 (a) 20   (b) 1   (c) 14   (d) 50
(e) 32   (f) 6   (g) 10   (h) 8
(i) 10   (j) 2   (k) 14   (l) 32
(m) 8   (n) 16

2 (a) 5.33    (b) 3.9    (c) 2.1
(d) 329    (e) 14.4    (f) $^-$2.5
(g) 40    (h) 90

## Practice booklet

### Section A (p 87)

1 (a) 6   (b) 11   (c) 17   (d) 6
(e) 11   (f) 7   (g) 13   (h) 1
(i) 3

2 (a) 11   (b) 4   (c) 6   (d) 6
(e) 12   (f) 6   (g) 3   (h) 14
(i) 5

3 (a) $24 \div 4 \times 2$    (b) $24 - 4 \times 2$
(c) $24 - 4 \div 2$    (d) $24 + 4 \times 2$

4 (a) Right    (b) Wrong, 18
(c) Wrong, 25    (d) Right
(e) Right    (f) Wrong, 7

## Section B (p 88)

1 (a) 18   (b) 15   (c) 4   (d) 3
(e) 15   (f) 2   (g) 4   (h) 5
(i) 8

2 (a) 15   (b) 19   (c) 11   (d) 2
(e) 11   (f) 3   (g) 8   (h) 19
(i) 2

3 **B** $2 \times (5 + 3)$    **C** $8 \times (5 - 3)$
**E** $(1 + 3) \times 4$

4 A and F, B and H, C and G, D and E

5 Expressions A, B, D and E do not need brackets.

## Section C (p 89)

1 (a) $12 + \dfrac{6}{2}$    (b) $\dfrac{12}{6} + 2$
(c) $\dfrac{12 + 6}{2}$    (d) $\dfrac{12}{6 + 2}$

2 A and G, B and H, C and E, D and F

3 (a) 4   (b) 12   (c) 3   (d) 8
(e) 4   (f) 17   (g) 5   (h) 4
(i) 16

## Sections D and E (p 89)

1 (a) 14.84    (b) 20.048    (c) 6.22
(d) 0.2115    (e) 17.885    (f) 26.5

2 (a) B    (b) F    (c) C
(d) E    (e) A    (f) D

3 (a) 20    (b) 3.2    (c) 14.3
(d) 6    (e) 24.3    (f) 6.5
(g) 7.5    (h) 8.5    (i) 27

4 (a) 3.5    (b) 5.25    (c) 5.1
(d) 8.46    (e) 1.4    (f) 3.62
(g) 0.04    (h) 0.59    (i) 3.48

5 (a) (i) 2.27 kg   (ii) 63.50 kg
(iii) 2.95 kg
(b) 1.2 pounds, 0.68 kg, 9 pounds, 4.09 kg, 4.5 kg

## Sections F and G (p 91)

1  (a)  196        (b)  841        (c)  16 384
   (d)  640 000    (e)  20.25      (f)  174.24
   (g)  0.25       (h)  10.1761

2  225, 256, 289 ($15^2$, $16^2$, $17^2$)

3  (a)  1521 ($39^2$)      (b)  1369 ($37^2$)

4  (a)  21   (b)  51   (c)  1.7   (d)  0.47

5  (a)  63   (b)  42   (c)  3.5   (d)  13.1

6  (a)  18   (b)  4.5   (c)  47

7  Yes, 26 stones

*8

## Sections H and I (p 92)

1  (a)  25   (b)  3    (c)  36   (d)  12
   (e)  4    (f)  10   (g)  16   (h)  4

2  (a)  0.74       (b)  6561      (c)  14.06
   (d)  0.092      (e)  ⁻7.3      (f)  6.9
   (g)  11.6       (h)  500       (i)  2

# Review 4 (p 206)

1  (a)  £4.80           (b)  £4.20
   (c)  Group A had the highest mean so it
        could be said to have done better.

2  (a)  ⁻4, ⁻3, ⁻2, 1, 5

   (b)  (i)  5 + ⁻3
        (ii)  ⁻4 + ⁻2
        (iii) ⁻4 + 1

3  (a)  (i)   Reflection in the vertical axis
        (ii)  Translation 2 units right,
              6 units down
        (iii) Rotation of 180° about (1, ⁻3)

   (b)  (i)   Reflection in the horizontal axis
        (ii)  Rotation of 180° about (0, 0)
        (iii) Translation 2 units left,
              6 units up

4  (a)  3, 6, 9, 15, 24

   (b)  1, 3, 6

   (c)  3, 17

   (d)  1, 9

5  (a)  (5, ⁻1)          (b)  (0, ⁻5)
   (c)  (⁻3, 3)          (d)  (1, ⁻1)

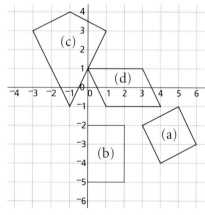

6  (a)  ⁻3           (b)  7           (c)  3

**7**

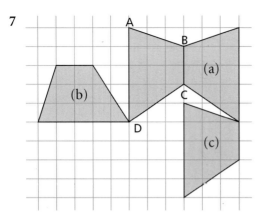

**8** (a) The numbers in the second row of the table are 5, 7, 9, 11, 13, 15, 17

    (b) Graph of $d = 2t + 5$ (a straight line from (0, 5) to (6, 17))

    (c) 12 metres

    (d) $1\frac{1}{2}$ minutes

    (e) $d = 2t + 5$

**9** (a) 20         (b) 4

**10** (a) The pupil's graphs of $y = x + 3$, $y = 2x$, $y = 8 - x$, $y = 2x + 1$

    (b) $y = 2x$ and $y = 2x + 1$

**11** (a) 19   (b) 6    (c) 1    (d) 18

**12** (a) Wednesday    (b) 12 degrees

    (c) 0.1°C

**13** (a) 5           (b) 25

    (c) 2482        (d) 99.28

**14** (a) 106    (b) 0.6     (c) 2.56

**15** (a) (i) 18.5    (ii) 12    (iii) 13

    (b) The mode or median best represents the age of the group.

    Over 80% of the group is younger than the mean of 18.5 years so the mean is not the most representative.

---

**Mixed questions 4** (Practice booklet p 95)

**1** (a) 12°C is **2** degrees higher than 10°C.

    (b) ⁻**2**°C is 8 degrees higher than ⁻10°C.

    (c) ⁻8°C is 4 degrees higher than ⁻**12**°C

    (d) ⁻4°C is 4 degrees **lower** than 0°C

**2** (a) 4         (b) 4.8       (c) 8

**3** (a) (8, 1), (5, ⁻4), (⁻2, ⁻2), (⁻1, 2)

    (b) 5 units right, one unit up

**4** (a) 16   (b) ⁻2   (c) ⁻1   (d) 0

**5** (a) $r = 7$  (b) $z = ⁻5$  (c) $s = 2$  (d) $v = ⁻2$

**6** (a) $\frac{6}{8}$ or $\frac{3}{4}$     (b) $\frac{4}{8}$ or $\frac{1}{2}$     (c) $\frac{4}{8}$ or $\frac{1}{2}$

    (d) $\frac{2}{8}$ or $\frac{1}{4}$     (e) $\frac{1}{8}$         (f) 0

**7**

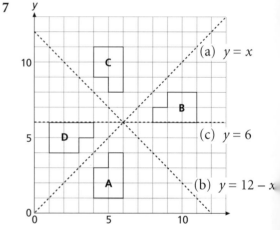

    (a) $y = x$

    (c) $y = 6$

    (b) $y = 12 - x$

    (d) Quarter turn anticlockwise, centre (6, 6)

**8** (a) 30         (b) 3

**9**

| 4 | 2 |
|---|---|
| 1 | 3 |

**10**

| 10 | 30 |
|----|----|
| 14 | 42 |

**11**

| 6 | 18 |
|---|----|
| 24 | 48 |

**12**

| 2 | 1 |
|---|----|
| 5 | 10 |

**13**

| 12 | 3 | 72 |
|----|---|----|
| 20 | 15 | 40 |
| 4 | 1 | 8 |

**14**

| 7 | 1 | 35 |
|----|----|----|
| 11 | 33 | 55 |
| 17 | 3 | 5 |